I0057204

INVEST

IN STOCK, BONDS, EFTS AND MUTUAL FUNDS

Innovation
Branding
Solution
Marketing

Shyam Bahadur, Professor
Iowa State University Ames, Iowa
Fellow A S M E and A S T M

INVESTING

In Stocks, ETFs and
Mutual Funds

(Investor's Guide to Building Wealth)

SHYAM BAHADUR, PROFESSOR
Iowa State University, Ames, Iowa Fellow
ASME and ASTM

Copyright © 2025 by Shyam Bahadur

All rights reserved. No part of this publication may be reproduced, distributed, or transmitted in any form or by any means, including photocopying, recording, or other electronic or mechanical methods, without the prior written permission of the copyright owner and the publisher, except in the case of brief quotations embodied in critical reviews and certain other noncommercial uses permitted by copyright law. For permission requests, write to the publisher, addressed "Attention: Permissions Coordinator," at the address below.

Books Academy LLC
112 SW HK Dodgen Loop,
Temple, Texas 76504
Hotline: (254) 800-1189

Ordering Information:

Quantity sales. Special discounts are available on quantity purchases by corporations, associations, and others. For details, contact the publisher at the address above.

Printed in the United States of America.

ISBN-13: Softcover   978-1-966567-57-8
              eBook   978-1-966567-58-5

To my wife for her

patience and sacrifice

PREFACE TO THE FIRST EDITION

The purpose of this book is to provide an understanding of the investments so that a beginner can get started and learn more and more progressively through direct involvement. There is a vast amount of material in both the published form and on the internet sites but a beginner does not know where to start. Often the material is presented in such a manner and detail that the learning process becomes overwhelming. Whereas this material is valuable for in-depth and broad understanding of the investments, it discourages the uninitiated to get started. The material presented in this book takes this into consideration and covers the topics in such a manner and depth that is usually enough to get started with minimal risk. Once a person gets started, the real perspective and general understanding follow to broaden the scope of investments in terms of the increasing levels of risk and greater return potential. With the comfort level so achieved, the desire of the person to build wealth over lifetime for a secure and happy retirement and for transfer to younger generations will assure life-long involvement in investing.

In keeping with the objective outlined above, the aim is to present the necessary material in steps based on the sound principles. The reader is prompted to make the investment in stages and see the accruing benefit while progressing to learn more and more. As for the investment, it may be real or phantom in the beginning. The idea is to build confidence through direct involvement and observation of the results. With this approach, the comfort level of the reader will increase with time. The progression of investments will be recommended on the basis of the real needs of the family at different stages of life. As the needs change, so will the nature of investments. It is hoped that this approach will inspire the reader and turn him/her into an astute practical investor.

The book covers all kinds of investments: certificates of deposits, treasury securities, bonds, stocks, mutual funds and exchange traded funds. A brief mention is made of the master limited partnerships and the real estate investment trusts as well. Associated with wealth building is the taxation which is also included in discussion. However, we need to understand that the tax laws change with time and so any discussion of the taxes is not going to be current. The objective of this discussion is merely to make the investor aware that the taxes have to be paid on dividends and capital gains. With the knowledge of the taxes, the investor can time the sale of the investments to minimize the tax burden.

The investor needs to understand that, when it comes to investing, there are no guarantees of profit. You may be an astute investor but have no control on the profits and losses of the businesses that you selected for investment. Often the outcome of investing is that you end up with profits in some and losses in others. The aim is to have more profits than losses and so the result is net profit. That is why diversification is considered necessary in investing.

Happy investing!

Shyam Bahadur

January 2018

PREFACE TO THE SECOND EDITION

The book has been revised with the original emphasis in mind of helping the reader to learn the basic concepts of stock market investing. In addition to the many small changes throughout the book, Chapter 3 on the Measures for Stock Valuation has been drastically revised. In Chapter 5 on the Selection and Analysis of Stocks for Investment, the expanded use of the brokerage internet site is demonstrated. It makes the process expedient without the need for searching the relevant data from various sources. Chapter 15 with the title "The Road to Wealth" has been added to inspire the reader to start investing finally if not already done so. I am confident that with du0.e diligence the reader will become proficient in investing in all kinds of instruments namely stocks, bonds, mutual funds and exchange traded funds. It is the diligence that leads to success in any endeavor and investing is no different.

Shyam Bahadur

February 2021

PREFACE TO THE THIRD EDITION

The book has been revised to make it easier and more useful in the selection of stocks using the information provided on the internet brokerage websites. With the guidance and information provided on these sites the selection of stocks has become easier and straightforward even for the beginners. This has reduced the complexity and the time for the collection of data needed for fundamental analysis. The chapter on the exchange traded funds has been expanded in view of their increased usage and popularity. In Chapter 7 the discussion of artificial intelligence and the industries related to them has been added. In addition to these additions, many other changes have been incorporated to make the book current and useful for the beginning and the

seasoned investors.

Shyam Bahadur

July 2024

List of Contents

Chapter 1

Investments as the Key to Wealth

1.1 Introduction

This chapter stresses the need for the accumulation of wealth and so provides the motivation for investing. It introduces the types of investments that are available. It encourages investing as early as possible by introducing the magic of compounding. It prompts the reader to invest on a regular basis so as to benefit from dollar cost averaging. It discusses the need for insurance, cash reserves and investing in the framework of budget. It provides an introduction to the tax-deferred accounts and emphasizes the benefits of these accounts.

1.2 Managing Your Money

Would you want to be a millionaire? Who wouldn't?

The question then is how to become a millionaire. Well, you could win a lottery but what are the odds. Alternatively, you could land a high-paying job like that of a CEO in a company. But then how many people have the qualifications and the luck to reach that level. In reality, a person with modest income can achieve financial prosperity only through regular savings and investing those savings in a prudent manner. This approach will help you in achieving the goal of decent living and prepare you for a comfortable retirement. Your success in this endeavor will depend upon your personal situation governed by the needs of your family and your regular income. The important thing to note here is that that you will need to motivate yourself to set aside a part of your income for investing and then invest this money regularly. The latter requires that you learn the basic investing principles which are covered in this book.

Most people have checking accounts in banks or credit unions. These are meant to facilitate the deposit of checks and payment of bills. The interest in a checking account is negligible and so this is not suitable as an investment. You can earn a slightly higher interest in a savings account or a money market account but these interest rates are also fairly small. The certificates of deposit (CDs) issued by the banks and the credit unions are much better in terms of the return but unlike the above accounts the money is locked for a specified period of time. These are safe because they carry FDIC (Federal Deposit Insurance) guarantee and have provided decent returns in the past). The certificates of deposit are ideal for investment where the money is intended to be used in a specific time frame such as the down payment on a home or the educational expenses of a child.

Other forms of investments involve risk. These are described in the next section. The objective of these investments is to enable your money to grow by a reasonable amount over a period of time even accounting for the income taxes and inflation. The understanding of these strategies and the associated risks is necessary for prudent investing.

1.3 Types of Investments

The term investment refers to the commitment of funds in instruments that will help to prevent the loss of purchasing power of money from inflation over a period of time. This is amply demonstrated by the fact that a car that cost $3,000 in the year 1975 would cost today in excess of $25,000.

Similarly, a home that cost $25,000 then would cost more than $100,000 today. So if you have $10,000 today saved for retirement, its purchasing power at the time of your retirement 40 – 50 years later would be much less and certainly not enough to take care of your needs in retirement. The only solution to the loss of your purchasing power of money over a period of time is investing it for appreciation.

The major categories of such investments are fixed deposits, bonds, common stocks, mutual funds and exchange traded funds which are discussed in detail in the following chapters. In order to integrate them in our discussion, the simple explanations of these terms are provided below:

1. Fixed Deposits- As the name implies, here the money is locked in these deposits for a predetermined period of time at a fixed rate that depends upon the time period. Normally the longer the period, the higher is the rate of return. Such deposits are commonly made in the banks, credit unions and other financial institutions. There is a penalty in case of early withdrawals if needed.

2. Bonds – These are issued by various agencies such as the US treasury and other federal agencies, state governments, municipal entities, and corporations. These agencies in effect borrow funds from the investors by selling bonds and have the obligation to pay interest on the bonds as well as the principal on maturity. Because of the borrowing nature, bonds are called debt obligations.

3. Common stocks – These represent the proportional ownership in a company. So if you purchase one hundred shares of a company which has one million shares of common stock, your share of the ownership in the company is 100/1,000,000. The common stocks entitle the stockholders the voting rights in proportion to the ownership of stock on major issues including the election of the company directors. The stockholder gets paid the dividend, if any, and benefits from the appreciation in stock price of the company if its profits increase and/or growth potential increases. In terms of the liability, the stockholder merely suffers from the drop in stock price if the company does not do well.

4. Mutual funds – They pool money from a large number of investors which is invested by the professional managers in stocks, bonds or any combination thereof, as the charter of the fund may dictate. In lieu of their investments, the investors are given shares which represent the proportional ownership in the fund. Thus the investors share the dividend and the appreciation or depreciation in the value of the fund.

5. Exchange traded funds – They are just like mutual funds in respect of the collection of funds from a large number of investors to invest. They invest generally in the specific narrower

segments of the market, are not actively managed and trade like stocks on the exchanges.

6. There are other kinds of investments possible also. For example, one can invest in rental real estate but this will require big investment needed to purchase the rental property. Alternatively, one may invest in real estate investment trusts (known as REITs) which trade like stocks. These do not require large investments.

Sophisticated investors also participate in options, futures, precious metals and collectibles. These are risky instruments and are not suitable for ordinary investors. As such these will not be included in our discussion in this book. In other words, the discussion in this book will be limited to stocks, bonds, mutual funds and exchange-traded funds which are commonly used for investing purposes.

1.4 The Need for Investing

In addition to safeguard against the loss of purchasing power of money as indicated above, we need to invest money for many other purposes some of which are given below:

1. Accumulate funds for children's education.
2. Make a down payment on home purchase.
3. Make purchases of big-ticket items such as cars, appliances, etc.
4. Pay bills related to medical charges, breakdowns, home repairs, insurance, real estate taxes, etc.
5. Take care of the living expenses in rough times such as unemployment and other financial emergencies.
6. Ability to take family vacations.
7. Support charitable causes.
8. Accumulate funds for the comfortable living in retirement.

We commonly read in newspapers and hear on radio and television news the stories of people who are overstretched on their credit card bills or have lost their homes because they could not afford the monthly mortgage payments. They have been forced into bankruptcy because of high medical bills or other unexpected emergencies. They have lost their jobs and are unable to support their families even with the unemployment benefits. In many cases, such hardships could have been avoided if people limited their expenditures and invested the savings for such contingencies. As for the retirement, some people think that social security payments will be adequate to take care of their needs in retirement years. This is certainly not the case. What is the solution? Save enough money and invest it wisely. This book will help you in doing this.

1.5 Preparing for a Secure Financial Future

Saving money for investing takes a lot of discipline and thoughtful planning. We have so many demands on the money that we earn. These involve the necessities such as food, housing, medical, clothing and transportation as well as the discretionary items such as recreation and travel, etc. In view of this, the following measures are recommended:

1. Pay off your debt as the first priority. Many people manage their lives with credit cards that carry very high interest rates often in excess of 20%. The use of credit cards is good strictly from the point of convenience so long as the balances are paid in full every month. If you regularly pay only the minimum amount required, it will be terrible for your finances because the interest accumulated will be too high and that will bury you under debt.

2. Consider having a term life insurance if you are married and/or have dependent children. Insurance industry provides universal life insurance which has a death benefit as well as an investment component. The investment part is not a good deal because you can do much better by investing on your own. So buy only the death benefit insurance which is called the term life insurance and invest the saving in insurance premium on your own.

3. Build some cash reserves for the following needs:

   a. The extra co-pay on medical bills, repairs in home, appliance break-down, car repairs, purchase of the items such as appliance, television, furniture, car, etc.

b. For a few months of expenses in case you or your spouse gets laid off.

4. Set aside some money for investing on a regular basis.

1.6 Time to Start Investing and the Magic of Compounding

Anytime is a good time to start investing. However, the earlier you do, the better it is. The reason for this is compounding. What it means is that $1,000 invested at 6% compound interest will grow to $2,012.20 in 12 years. In another 12 years, it will grow to $4,048.90 and in the next 12 years to $8,147.30. It means that if we make our initial investment of $1,000 at the age of 29 years, we will end up with more than $8,000 at the age of 65 years. This magic of multiplying the money to more than eight times in 36 years is due to compounding because we are getting the return on the money earned in our account year after year. *This is the simple and the most important* rule *of wealth accumulation: the earlier you start investing, the more you are going to have in terms of the wealth at the end.*

Most people start working full-time after completing their education at the age of 25 years. They have thus a span of 40 years for investing till they reach a presumed retirement age of 65 years. Table 1.1 illustrates the accumulation of wealth that would result if $3,000 is invested every year over this period. Included in the table are also the accumulated values for 20 and 30 years for those people who could have started investing later or retired earlier. We include here three yearly rates of compound return, namely 5%, 9%, and 11%. A return of 5% is achievable from fixed income investments such as the combination of certificates of deposit and bonds, 8-10% from stocks invested over a long period of time, and 10-12% by the smart do-it-yourself investors.

Table 1.1 Accumulation in $ by investing $3,000 yearly at the compound rates of return of 5%, 9% and 11%.

Amount invested per year	No. of years invested	Accumulation at 5% return	Accumulation at 9% return	Accumulation at 11% return
$3000	20	$112,118	$184,107	$237,982
$3000	30	$222,248	$485,529	$731,417
$3000	40	$401,639	$1,199,104	$2,132,484

The results of the accumulated returns are staggering in the sense that $3000 invested per year at 9% compound rate of return over a period of 40 years would grow to more than one million dollars. The same amount invested regularly over the same period at 11% compound rate of return accumulates to more than 2.132 million dollars. What this tells us is that a person of modest income can become a millionaire by starting to invest early and doing so on a regular basis.

As expected, the higher rate of return would result in a larger accumulation for any period. For example, $3000 invested yearly at 5% compound return results in the accumulation of $112,118 over 20 years (as in Table 1.1) whereas at 10% compound return it will grow to $209,190 for the same period. If instead of doubling the rate of return, the years of accumulation are doubled, say from 20 to 40 years, the accumulated values then for 5% rate of return are $112,118 for 20 years and $401,639 for 40 years (Table 1.1). This tells us that by doubling the rate of return the accumulation is less than double but by doubling the number of years the accumulation is roughly quadrupled. In other words, *the period of accumulation is more important than the rate of return for accumulation of wealth*. Please note that as an investor we do not have control on the rate of return but we can certainly make sure that we start investing as early as possible. *This is the cardinal rule of investing*.

1.7 Dollar Cost Averaging

It refers to investing the same amount on a regular basis which may be a set interval such as a month, quarter, year or any combination thereof. Dollar cost averaging is possible with any kind of investment but is most suited for mutual funds because one can invest as low as $50 with some mutual funds and the amount may be taken out of the investor's account at the specified regular intervals. The mutual fund buys the shares of the fund at the current share price and these are deposited in the investor's account. Since the fund share prices fluctuate on a daily basis, you buy more shares for the same amount invested when the prices are low than when they are high. This tends to average out the fluctuation in price and so is called dollar cost averaging. *It is another cardinal rule of investing.*

1.8 Investing in Tax-deferred Accounts

Taxes are an important consideration in investing because they reduce the money that we get to keep. In a normal (taxable) account, both the state and the federal taxes are paid on the dividends as well as the capital gains resulting from the sale of the shares. On the contrary, in tax-deferred accounts the money grows tax-deferred until the account holder reaches a particular age, 70-1/2 years currently, when withdrawals are mandatory. These withdrawals from tax-deferred accounts are taxed at the rates applicable to short-term investments, defined as those held for a year or less.

Since the tax-deferred accounts allow for tax-free growth over the years, one should give priority to investing for retirement in such accounts over the taxable accounts.

The tax-deferred plans available to working and business class people are 401(k) and 403(b). In these plans, a person can elect to defer receiving a portion of the salary which is instead contributed on his or her behalf, before taxes, to the plan. There are special rules governing the operation of such plans which may change from time to time. For example, there is a dollar limit on the amount a person may elect to defer each year, thereby saving on taxes in that year. Some employers add to this contribution on behalf of the employee which makes the investment even more appealing. Since the rules governing such accounts change from time to time, one should refer to the US Department of Labor website http://www.dol.gov/. If you are employed, the Personnel Department of your employer can provide you the necessary guidance.

As a retirement benefit, the businesses offer the Employee Stock Ownership Plan (ESOP) which is a form of defined contribution plan in which the investments are primarily in the company stock. The details of these retirement benefit plans are also available on the above website. The retirement benefit options available for the self-employed business owners are *Keogh plans, Simplified Employee Pensions, and Simple plans*. The details of these plans are available on the US Chamber of Commerce website http://business.uschamber.com/P08/P08_4800.asp.

In addition to the above plans, the government allows tax-deferred investment of a part of your earned income in Individual Retirement Account (IRA). There are two kinds of IRAs: traditional and Roth. The investment in Roth IRA is from after-tax earnings and the accumulations are tax-free. In traditional IRA the tax payer is allowed the deduction of the amount contributed to IRA from the earned income. This provides the account holder the benefit of tax saving at this stage. However, unlike Roth IRA (which is never taxed), traditional IRA is subject to mandatory withdrawals at the age of 70-1/2 year currently and the capital gains on these withdrawals are taxed at the (higher) short- term capital gains rates. The amounts allowed for IRAs have changed from time to time and are also dependent upon the income and age limits. IRA accounts of both kinds can be opened and maintained at a bank or brokerage of your choice and they provide you the freedom to select the investments of your choice as well. For current information on IRAs, refer to the website http://business.uschamber.com/P08/P08_4820.asp.

It should be noted that the investments in tax-deferred accounts have restrictions in terms of the investment amount as well as the withdrawal age, the latter being so because they are intended solely for retirement. In addition to this, one should consider investing in taxable accounts so as to supplement the accumulation in retirement funds. For the obvious benefit of tax-deferral, one should give priority to investing in tax-deferred accounts to the maximum amount allowed by law.

1.9 Summary

1. The purpose of investing is to allow the money to grow over a period of time.
2. The goal of investing is to prepare for the major financial needs

such as child's education, home purchase, home repairs, purchase of big -ticket items and retirement.

3. The traditional forms of investments for the long haul are stocks, bonds, mutual funds and exchange traded funds.

4. It is possible to start investing in stock and bond mutual funds with small amounts of money.

5. It is to the advantage of the investor to start investing as early as possible so as to derive the maximum benefit from compounding.

6. One should maximize investing in the tax-deferred accounts before starting to invest in the taxable accounts.

7. It is a good practice to invest on a regular schedule (monthly, quarterly, yearly, etc.).

Suggested Action Items

1. If employed, make sure that you participate in the employee benefit programs such as (401) k and (403) b (See section 1.8).

2. Contribute to Roth IRA, if eligible, which allows tax-free accumulation and withdrawal. If not contribute to traditional IRA which allows tax-free accumulation.

3. Start building cash reserves for emergencies and for the purchase of big -ticket items.

4. Start investing on a regular basis so to benefit from compounding.

Chapter 2

Basics of Stock Market Investing

2.1 Introduction

This chapter introduces the concept of public and private companies and that the shareholder is the part owner of a public company. The investing in the stock market means buying the share of a company traded on the stock exchange. It talks about the stock price and how it is affected by a host of factors. It introduces the terminology related to stock market investing such as the ticker symbol, stock price, stock exchanges and stock market indexes, etc. It describes the characterization of stocks in terms of the value, growth and income, common and preferred, large, mid and small caps, etc. It explains the terms applicable to the trading of common stocks.

2.2 Investing in The Stock Market

When we invest in the stock market, we do so by buying the shares of a company that trades on a stock exchange. Such a company is known as the *public* company. A company that is not open to the public for trading is called a *private* company. You may have heard people saying that they would like to have their own company or business. A company like this is a private company and is not open to the public. When a private company has established the track record of operations and built some equity, it may be brought in the open market by issuing an IPO which is known as the *initial public ofering*. This is a process by which shares of the private company are sold to the public at a price which is arrived at by looking at the equity, business prospects and profit potential. The major reason for taking the company to the open market is to have the ability to raise capital for use in the operation, development and expansion of the business of the company.

Now the company becomes a public company and is accountable to the Securities and Exchange Commission which is an agency that regulates the companies listed on the stock exchanges. The latter provide market for the exchange of shares between the buyers and the sellers.

By purchasing the shares of a public company, you become a part owner of the company. Your ownership interest in the company is given by the ratio of the number of shares owned by you to the total number of shares of the company. For most people, this ratio is very small considering that the companies have many millions of shares outstanding. The company has a Board of Directors which makes major policy decisions and a Chief Executive Officer (CEO) who is responsible for the execution of these policies along with the normal functioning of the company. The Board of Directors is elected by the shareholders and, as a part owner of the company, your vote counts. In practice, your vote may not affect much unless you are a major shareholder of the company. Being part owner of the company, you stand to be affected by the performance of the company. If the company does well in terms of the revenue generation and the profits, it would be expected to result in the appreciation of its stock price. This will increase the value of your investment in the company stock. On the other hand, if the company performs poorly, its stock price will suffer and this will decrease the value of your investment in the company.

2.3 Factors Affecting the Stock Price

The price of a stock fluctuates with time. The fluctuation in price is caused by the changes in supply and demand. In the stock market, there are always buyers and sellers; the only variable is the price of the stock. If the investors think that the stock price should be higher than its current price as perceived based on the fundamentals and the earnings prospects of the company, they will be willing to pay a higher price. This will raise the price of the stock. On the other hand, a negative outlook for the company will push the price of stock lower. Note that for every transaction there is a seller and a corresponding buyer. Thus, if there is positive news for the company, there are more buyers and fewer sellers and this changes the supply and demand relationship. In this scenario, the price of stock will go up to entice more sellers so as to balance the supply and demand equation. The same works in the opposite direction when there is bad news.

Some of the key factors that move the price of a specific stock up or down are listed below:

1. The company reports earnings per share for the past quarter which is above or below the analyst estimates.
2. The up or down guidance of the company for the revenues and earnings for the next quarter and the year.
3. The company announces a new discovery or product which has the potential to increase earnings in future.
4. The company announces a new reorganization which is expected to increase the efficiency and hence the earnings.
5. The company announces the appointment of a key top management, such as the CEO or the Financial Officer, who has the track record of steering the business into a more profitable enterprise. Sometimes this may have temporarily a negative effect because of the uncertainty factor associated with the new appointment.
6. A market report which is positive or negative for the products of the company and the competition.
7. Changes in the price of a commodity such as oil, metals, chemicals, etc. which can affect the earnings of the company.
8. An analyst or a brokerage issues a report which may be positive or negative.

In addition to the above, there are larger macroeconomic factors such as employment rate, GDP, inflation, geopolitical risks etc. (see chapter 14) that affect the stock market as a whole.

2.4 Ticker Symbol

In order to facilitate trading, the stocks of public companies are listed on a stock exchange. The latter is the marketplace where stocks of the companies are traded, that is bought and sold. Each company is assigned a unique ticker symbol and the trading of the stock is done using this ticker symbol. The following are the examples of the ticker symbols for some companies:

Ticker Symbol	Company Name
C	Citigroup
F	Ford Motor
GILD	Gilead Sciences
MSFT	Microsoft
CL	Colgate
RIG	Palmolive Transocean

The trading sites help you to find the ticker symbol when the name of the company is entered in the space provided.

2.5 Stock Exchanges

The stocks of the companies are traded on the stock exchanges. The companies that issue stock for public trading apply for listing on these exchanges. In the USA the following three stock exchanges are there:

1. New York Stock Exchange (NYSE)
2. American Stock Exchange (AMEX)
3. National Association of Securities Dealers Automated Quotation (NASDAQ) system (also called OTC which stands for over-the-counter trading).

NYSE and AMEX used to be the auction markets in which brokers represented both the buyers and the sellers who negotiated the best price possible for transaction. These two exchanges were located in New York. In contrast to these exchanges, NASDAQ was a fully computerized exchange where market makers conducted transactions through an electronic network of terminals. NASDAQ did not have a physical floor and so was called the over-the-counter (OTC) market, unlike the NYSE and AMEX which had physical floors. With the advent of computers, all trading is done now using the computers as opposed to the floor trading and limited trading also takes place during off hours.

The exchanges open at 9.30 am and close at 4.00 pm Eastern Standard Time.

2.6 Listing Requirements on the Stock Exchanges

In order for the company stock to be listed on a specific exchange, the companies have to meet the following requirements:

1. NYSE - The listing requirements for this exchange are that the company has at least 1.1 million shares of the common stock owned by the shareholders, pre-tax profits of at least $10 million over the last three years, and a global market capitalization of at least $40million. If at any time the listed company falls short of these requirements, it is dropped from on the exchange.

2. AMEX – This exchange is much smaller than the NYSE exchange. Its listing requirements are $0.5 million shares of the common stock outstanding, total market capitalization of at least $4 million, and the annual pre-tax income of $0.75 million or more.

3. NASDAQ - Its listing requirements are a minimum of 2,200 shareholders, 1.25 million shares of the outstanding stock worth $70 million, and the pre-tax profit of $11 million over the last three years. A large number of the technology companies in sizes much larger than the requirement are listed on this exchange.

In addition to the above three major exchanges, there are five regional exchanges: Philadelphia, Boston, Cincinnati, Chicago and the Pacific Exchange. These exchanges are used for the listing of stocks of local companies. Some company stocks are dual listed, that is both on a main exchange as well as a regional exchange.

2.7 Stock Market Indexes

The important news of interest to the investing community is "How did the stock market do today?" The answer to the above question lies in the performance of the stock market indexes. The three indexes most commonly used are:

1. Dow Jones Industrial Average (DJIA)
2. Standard & Poor 500 Composite Index (S&P 500)
3. NASDAQ

DJIA index is computed from 30 leading stocks chosen by the Dow Jones & Company to represent different industries. This average is composed of *the blue-chip companies*, meaning large, well-established and well-known companies. It is a price-weighted average index which means that a high- priced stock carries more weight than a low-priced stock. For example, a 10 % change in the price of a $100 stock equals $10 while the same 10 % percent change in the price of a $50 stock equals $5. Thus, in the $15 total change, the contribution of the higher-priced stock is more than that of the lower-priced stock even though both had the same 10 % change.

S&P 500 index is considered to be more representative of the stock market performance than the DJIA index. It is so because the S&P 500 index tracks the performance of 500 companies from different segments such as the manufacturing, financial, utility, consumer durables, transportation, technology, etc. and is a capitalization-weighted index. The capitalization of a company is worked out by multiplying the number of shares outstanding with the stock price. Thus S&P 500 index is influenced more by the size of the company than the DJIA index. This index is more representative of the market because it is based on the larger number of companies and that too from more segments of the market.

The National Association of Security Dealers has several indexes for the market segments such as the industrials, banks, transportation, insurance, biotechnology, telecommunications and computers. All of these indexes are combined in a composite index known as the NASDQ index. This index is heavily dominated by the stocks of technology companies such as Apple, Applied Materials, Microsoft, Cisco, Dell, Intel and others.

In addition to the above three indexes, there are many other indexes used by the investment community. These are the S&P 100, S&P Midcap 400, S&P Midcap 600, NASDAQ 100, NASDAQ Global Market Composite, Wilshire 5000, Russell 1000, Russell 2000, etc. Wilshire 5000 is the broadest index which includes both the large cap and small cap stocks. Russell 1000 index consists of large-cap stocks primarily. Russell 2000 is often cited as the index of small-cap stocks. In addition to these, there is the EAFE index which is the benchmark for foreign stocks.

It should be noted from the above discussion that the stock market indexes serve as the performance indicators of a particular segment of the stock market. They are particularly useful for comparing the performance of a specific portfolio. For example, mutual funds routinely compare the performance of their stock portfolio with the corresponding index.

2.8 Qualitative Characterization of Common Stocks

Some of the characterizations used for the common stocks are:

1. Blue chip stocks - These are the stocks of large and high-quality companies with stable businesses, long record of good earnings, and sound financial condition. They are considered relatively safe having good appreciation potential and are suited for core holdings in an investor's portfolio.

2. Growth stocks - These are the stocks of companies with high growth potential. Such companies pay small-to-no dividends and instead invest the profits in research and development to spur future growth. The capital appreciation potential of such companies is greater than that of the blue-chip companies but the associated risk is also greater. The growth stocks are preferred by aggressive investors looking for large capital appreciation.

3. Value stocks - These are the stocks of companies which have depressed stock prices because of the temporary problems in their business. Their valuations are normally lower than those of the growth stocks.

4. Cyclical stocks - These are the stocks of companies which have cyclical business characteristics. Such companies flourish when the economy is good and suffer when the economy is bad.

5. Defensive stocks - These are the stocks of companies which cater to the items of daily needs such as food and health-related products. In bad economic times, when the discretionary

spending is tight, such stocks are considered relatively safe.

6. Income stocks - These stocks pay good dividends but their appreciation potential is generally limited. Such stocks are popular with retirees and others who depend upon the dividend income for subsistence.

7. Speculative stocks - These are the stocks of budding companies with a high probability of failure. Such companies are still trying to establish and so their earnings are either nil or fairly small. They have investment appeal because, if successful, they have the potential for large capital appreciation. They are, however, risky investments. The speculative stocks with very low prices ($1 or less) are known as the *penny stocks* which trade in over-the- counter markets and pink sheets. *One should normally shy away from the penny stocks because of the high probability of failure of the associated businesses.*

8. Foreign stocks – As opposed to the domestic stocks, these are the stocks of companies located outside the country. Some of them are listed as the American Depository Receipts (ADRs) and they trade like the domestic stocks.

2.9 Classification of Stocks by Capitalization

The number of shares outstanding multiplied by the stock price of the company gives the capitalization of the company. Capitalization is thus indicative of the size of the company. In general, the larger and more established companies have larger capitalization while the smaller and newer companies have smaller capitalization. Based on the criterion of capitalization, the categories assigned to the stocks are large-cap, mid-cap, small-cap, micro-cap and nano-cap. With some variations, the categories of market capitalization are:

Large-cap	$10B plus
Mid-cap	$2B to $10B
Small-cap	$300m to $2B
Micro-cap	$50m to $300m
Nano-cap	Less than $50

Large-cap companies are considered to be more stable and safer for investment than the other companies. Mid-cap and small-cap companies are more dynamic than large-cap companies but are regarded to be riskier. Micro-cap companies are in the early stages of development and so are considered to be much riskier but more rewarding. Nano-cap stocks are too risky and should ordinarily be avoided.

2.10 Common Stocks versus Preferred Stocks

In addition to the common stocks, some companies have the preferred stocks

as well. The preferred stock is a sort of hybrid security having the characteristics of both an equity security and a fixed-income security. As for the equity security, it is like a common stock which pays dividend and has an infinite life. As for the fixed-income security, its dividend is fixed and so provides a steady income similar to that of a bond. This stream of income continues for ever unless the issue is called or retired. The fluctuations in the price of preferred stocks often exceed those in bonds and so the preferred stocks are more volatile than the bonds. Some preferred stocks carry the convertibility feature which entitles the stock holder to convert the preferred stock to the common stock at a predetermined price.

The preferred stocks have some preferences over the common stocks. Firstly, the holder of the preferred stock gets preference for the dividend being paid first before any dividend is paid on the common stock. Secondly, if the company goes in bankruptcy, the preferred stock holders are paid ahead of the common stock holders.

Sometimes a company may have a series of preferred stocks. The ticker symbols for the common stock and each of the series of preferred stocks are unique.

2.11 Opening an Account at a Brokerage Firm

In order to buy and sell stocks and other investment products, one needs to open an account with a brokerage firm. The latter provides services such as the purchase and sale of investment products and holding them in the account, the collection of dividends, and the maintenance of account. The latter provides an accounting of the stocks, bonds, and mutual funds in terms of the number and the prices of the shares bought and sold during the calendar year which is needed for tax accounting purposes.

There are two kinds of brokerage firms:

1. Full-service brokerages - Here you have an investment advisor (commonly called the *broker*) assigned to you. The broker will discuss your situation along with your investment goals. Consistent with these goals, he/she will discuss the investment products (stocks, bonds or mutual funds) and recommend them for purchase or sale. On your instructions, the broker will carry out the trade for you.

2. Discount brokerages (also called the *Internet brokers*) - Here you normally make the investment decisions on your own. The investment advice is typically available on their websites which an investor can use. Mainly the brokerage provides an electronic platform for the execution of trade. Here you place the order on your own and the trade is executed electronically. Some premier discount brokerages may provide limited advice on investments. Recently in October 2019 online brokerages started providing commission-free trading. The idea here is that with no commissions the investors will trade more which will generate more cheap cash in the investor's accounts. This could help the brokers to sell other services like wealth management or automated portfolio tools which would be more profitable.

At the end of the chapter in Appendix 2.1, a list of the discount and the full-service brokers is given along with their web addresses. Opening an account with a brokerage is fairly easy. Just download the application from the brokerage website, complete and mail. If needed, you may call the customer service on the phone number listed on its website for help in completing the application. When the account is opened, you access it with a password on the brokerage website.

2.12 How to Trade Stocks

The trading of stocks refers to buying or selling the shares of a company. In the case of full-service brokerage, you call your broker and direct him/her to buy or sell the specific number of shares of the particular company. In the case of discount brokerage, you do this on the brokerage site on your own. If needed, the help is available. The information needed for trading is the stock ticker symbol, the number of shares to buy or sell, and the acceptable trade price of the stock, as shown in Figure 2.1

Buy/Sell:
Shares
Symbol:

Order Type: Limit
Price: $ Duration:
Figure 2.1 Order entry layout

The first three entries are self-evident. The fourth entry refers to the Order Type. By clicking on the arrow on the right of order type, we get the following three choices:

1. Market Order - It is an order to buy or sell the stock immediately at the best available current price. This kind of order guarantees execution, but not the execution price. This is the most common type of order category normally used.

For every stock there is an **Ask price** and a **Bid price.** Note that the **Buy** market orders are executed generally at the **Ask** price while the **Sell** market orders are executed at the **Bid** price.

2. Limit Order - Here the order specifies to buy or sell shares at a set *limit* price. So the order type is 'Limit'. In this case, the limit price is entered in the space assigned for it. This is a conditional order as opposed to the 'Market Order' and so the execution of the order is not guaranteed because the stock may not trade at that price. Alternatively, only a limited number of shares may be traded at the set limit price in which case it will be a partial execution of the order. Limit orders are particularly suited for

stocks which trade in small amounts on a daily basis. Such stocks are normally subject to the large fluctuation in price with small volume transactions.

3. Stop Order - This is an order to buy or sell a stock when its price surpasses a particular point. At the designated price, the stop order becomes a market order. As such the trade in this case may occur at a price better or worse than the stop price.

The stop order is a useful tool to protect the profit in a stock in case a sudden drop in the price of stock occurs. For example, if you bought a stock for $20/share and it is now trading at $30/share, you have a profit of 50%. If the stock suddenly drops in price, you may lose some or all of the profit. You can protect yourself by placing a stop order to sell at $28/share so that at the moment the price of stock drops to $28/share, it becomes a market order resulting in selling the stock at $28 (or less in case the price drops during the execution). In a similar way, the stop order can also be used to limit the loss. For example, if you bought the stock at $20/share, you may place the stop order to sell at a lower price, say $16/share, in case the stock drops in price. This way the loss has been limited to $(20 - 16)/20 = 20\%$.

On the last line of Figure 2.1 is the duration. It specifies the time period for which the order is good. There are three choices: 'Today ', 'Good till date ' or 'Good until cancelled '. Today means good today until 4.00 PM Eastern Standard Time (EST) when active trading stops.

2.13 Summary

1. There are two types of companies: public and private. The public companies are traded on a stock exchange.

2. Investing in the stock market involves buying the shares of a public company and holding them with the expectation of price appreciation. Depending upon the changes in stock price, one may end up with profit or loss when the shares are sold.

3. The stock price is affected by a number of factors such as those listed in Section 2.3.

4. Any company listed on the stock exchange is assigned a unique symbol called the "ticker symbol" which is used for trading the

stock of the company.

5. The stocks of companies are listed on the main stock exchanges. In addition to the above, there are regional exchanges which are used for the listing of local companies.

6. The stocks of the companies in the early stages of development are traded on the pink sheets. Such companies are fairly risky because of the lack of profits and reliable information and should normally be avoided.

7. Stock market indexes such as the Dow Jones Industrial Average (DJIA), Standard & Poor 500 (S&P 500), and NASDQ are commonly used to describe the stock market performance. In addition to these popular indexes, there are other indexes as well, for example, S&P 100, S&P Midcap 400, S&P Midcap 600, NASDAQ 100, Wilshire 5000, Russell 1000, etc. Each of these is designed to indicate the performance of a particular segment of stocks.

8. In view of the investment characteristics, the common stocks are referred to as the blue-chip, growth, value, cyclical, defensive, income and speculative stocks.

9. In terms of the market capitalization, common stocks are referred to as the large cap, mid cap, small cap, micro cap and nano cap stocks.

10. Some companies issue the preferred stocks in addition to the common stocks. The preferred stock has a fixed dividend and trades like a common stock. As compared to the common stock, it has preferences in terms of the priority of dividend payment and redemption in the event of bankruptcy of the company.

11. Buying and selling of the stocks is done on the electronic platform of the stock exchange.

12. There are three kinds of orders: market order, limit order and stop order.

Suggested Action Items

1. Open an account at a brokerage and glance the kind of information available on the website.

2. Buy some shares with the ticker symbol SPY which tracks the Standard and Poor (S&P) 500 Index composed of the blue-chip companies. With this selection, you do not have to pick the particular companies for investment because your performance will depend upon the performance of the companies in the index. This is a safe and proven way to play the stock market. This will help in the following ways:

   (i) Get you invested in the stock market right away.

   (ii) Give you the feel of stock market investing by watching the prices go up and down.

   (iii) Prepare you psychologically to filter the noise and stay in the market for the long haul.

Appendix 2.1 List of full service and discount brokerages and their web addresses

(A) Full-Service Brokers

Raymond James	www.raymondjames.com
Edward Jones	www.edwardjones.com
Merrill Lynch	www.merrilllynch.com
Wachovia	www.wachoviasec.com
A.G. Edwards	www.agedwards.com
UBS	www.ubs.com
Morgan Stanley	www.morganstanley.com
Smith Barney	www.smithbarney.com

(B) Discount Brokers

Charles Schwab	www.schwab.com
Fidelity	www.fidelity.com
Bank of America	www.bankofamerica.com
Interactive Brokers	www.interactivebrokers.com
Merrill Edge	www.merrilledge.com
Muriel Siebert	www.siebertnet.com
Robinhood	www.robinhood.com
TradeKing	www.tradeking.com
TradeStation	www.tradestation.com

Chapter 3

Measures of Stock Valuation

3.1 Introduction

The aim of this chapter is to discuss the valuation of common stocks. The measures commonly used for valuation are introduced and discussed in the context of the selection of stocks for investment. The relevance of these measures is examined with reference to the financial website of a company. This leads to the introduction of many other variables that apply to the financial aspects of a company. The concepts and the understanding developed here are used in later chapters in the evaluation and the selection of stocks for investment.

3.2 The Need for Valuation

The considerations in buying a common stock are similar to those involved in buying any major item, say a car. Why would you consider buying a car? It is just because you need transportation. Similarly, why would you consider buying the common stock of a company? It is because you want to invest in the stock market to get a greater return on your money than what is available from other investments. While trying to narrow down the choice of a car, you are confronted with many choices such as the size, make and price of the car. In the size alone, there are many choices available such as the full size, medium size, and compact/subcompact sedans in addition to the wagons and the SUVs. The similar analogy applies to common stocks of the companies which may be large cap, medium cap or small cap and that too in the many business choices available. Now in every size of the car there are different makes and models available. So you need to examine the specifications in order to narrow down your choice of the most suitable make and model consistent with a good price.

As applied to the common stocks, the analogy relates to the different sectors and the companies in a particular sector. In other words, you need to narrow down your choice to a particular company whose stock is a good investment and a good fit in your portfolio consistent with your requirement of the income and/or capital appreciation. This requires the evaluation of stock by using the valuation measures discussed below. It is what forms the basis for the fundamental approach to stock evaluation.

3.3 Qualitative Valuation Measures

In this section, we introduce the quantitative measures for the evaluation of stock relative to the other companies in the same business or related businesses. In addition to this we need to know that the stock is rightly priced that is not overpriced relative to its past.

The following are the quantitative valuation measures used in the evaluation of stocks for investment. The accompanying discussion is provided to provide the understanding and relevance.

1. Earnings per share (E/sh)

Earnings are the most important part of any business. Earnings per share is thus an important valuation measure in stock evaluation. It equals the total earnings divided by the number of outstanding shares of the company. For the earnings valuation we need to look at the E/sh for the past few years, current year, and the estimated earnings for the next year. A company with the prospect of rising earnings is definitely worth exploring for investment. Note that the next year's earnings are based on the projected earnings which may vary from analyst to analyst.

The following points with respect to the earnings should be noted:

(a) earnings of the company are affected by the supply and demand of its products.

(b) The earnings of the cutting-edge companies may go down because the technological superiority may suffer or the competition may increase.

(c) A new legislation or approval may affect the pricing of the products of the company, something very common in drug industries.

(d) The company may enhance its earnings in a particular quarter through promotions, special incentives and credit financing which is common in the automobile business. This could affect adversely the earnings in the succeeding quarters.

(e) The analysts may increase the earnings estimates to justify the favorable **Buy** rating for the company.

2. Price to earnings ratio (P/E)

The most common measure used in the evaluation of a company is the P/E ratio which is the price of the stock divided by its earnings per share. Conceptually, P/E may be looked as being the price in $ that investors are willing to pay per unit earnings of the company.

Here one should keep in mind that the earnings of the company may change from year to year. Thus if we use the earnings per share for the current year, we get the current P/E ratio. Analysts often estimate the forward price of the company stock by multiplying the next year's estimated earnings per share with the current P/E or the estimated value of P/E based on the future potential of the company. The problem with this estimate is that it is as good as the numbers used in its calculation and so it may be quite a bit off the

mark. Additionally, P/E may be affected by the interest rate changes, having an inverse relationship. That is when interest rate decreases, P/E tends to increase and vice versa.

3. Relative P/E

This involves comparing the current P/E of the company with the current P/E of its competitors. Obviously, all other things being equal, the lower the PE of a company, the better it is for investment. It should be noted that some companies in the same industry trade historically at a premium to others.

Furthermore, the comparison of P/E is valid in the same industry group because the companies in different industries trade at different P/E ratios.

4. P/E to growth ratio (PEG)

PEG is an important ratio for a growth company and is defined as the P/E ratio of a company divided by its growth rate. The company is considered normally undervalued if its PEG is 1.5 or less.

5. Price/book ratio (P/B)

It is defined as the ratio of the price of the stock to its book value per share. The book value represents the intrinsic net worth of the company. Conceptually, it is the value that the shareholder would receive if the company was liquidated.

Similar to the PEG for a growth company, P/B is a good measure for a value company. The lower the P/B ratio of the company, the better value it is for investment. It should further be noted that the value stocks have lower P/B ratios than the growth stocks. The price/book ratio is an important valuation parameter particularly for the depressed companies.

6. Price/sales ratio (P/S)

It is the price of the stock divided by the sales revenue per share. Conceptually, it tells how much an investor is willing to pay for every dollar of sales by the company. The lower the P/S ratio for a company, the better it is for investment.

7. Price /free cash flow ratio (P/CF)

Free cash flow (CF) is the money left after all the bills including the capital expenditures have been paid out of the earnings of the company. Price-to-free cash flow ratio (P/CF) is the ratio of the stock price to its free cash flow per share. The higher the free cash flow, the more money is available to the company for investment in the business, stock buyback and dividend payment to the shareholders. Since high cash flow is desirable, the lower the price-to-free cash flow ratio, the better the company is considered for investment.

It should be noted that for evaluation purposes the free cash flow per share is considered to be a better measure than the sales per share. It is so because the sales may be inflated by selling the goods on credit but the free cash flow cannot be distorted because it is based on the money left after all the bills have been paid.

8. Return on equity (ROE)

The term 'equity' refers to the ownership in an asset in excess of the claims or the lien against it. For example, the equity in home equals the difference between the expected sale price and the outstanding loan amount. As for the business, equity refers to the real worth of the company. Thus the return on equity is the ratio of the net earnings of the business to its equity, and this is expressed as a percentage. Conceptually speaking, ROE gives the return earned per dollar invested in the business. Since the management has to do a lot with the return on equity, the latter is also an indicator of the management effectiveness.

9. Net profit margin

It is defined as the ratio of the profit earned to the total sales by the company. Thus if the profit is 10 million for a sales receipt of 100 million, the net profit margin is 10%. Obviously the higher the profit margin, the more profitable is the company.

It should be noted that the profit margin is dependent upon the type of industry. For example, the net profit margin in the technology company is much higher than in the food business. Thus this measure is useful for the comparative evaluation of the companies in the same business.

10. Debt/equity ratio

It is the ratio of the debt on the books of the company to its equity. Debt to equity ratio is an inverse indicator of the financial strength of the company. If the debt in comparison to the equity is large, the company runs the risk of not being able to pay its debt particularly in bad economic times and so the company may be forced to seek bankruptcy. In the case of bankruptcy, the stockholders' equity is wiped out, and so it is risky to invest in the companies with high debt/equity ratio.

11. Current ratio and Quick ratio

Both of the above ratios provide a measure of the ability of the business to pay for its current liabilities. These ratios are defined as below:

Current ratio = (Cash + Marketable securities + Receivables + Inventory)/Current liabilities

Quick ratio = (Cash + Marketable securities + Receivables)/Current liabilities

It should be noted that the difference between the above two ratios is merely of the inventory. Inventory is the questionable item to include in the liquidity analysis because it may be difficult to convert inventory into cash in the short term. So a more reliable and stringent measure of the short-term liquidity is the quick ratio.

3.4 Stock Quotation

With the understanding of the terms discussed above, we can now look at a typical stock quotation. You can get the stock quotation from your broker's website or any financial site such as http://finance.yahoo.com/, www.morningstar.com and others. You will need a brokerage account for trading privileges. I suggest that you do that with a discount brokerage listed in Appendix 2.1. Here you will be able to trade free of charges. Along with the trading privilege, the brokerage will provide you all kinds of financial data, research reports, account statement, collection of dividends, and tax forms at year end. If you are hesitant, you may dial the customer service and the staff will be very cooperative in helping you to set up the account.

Table 3.1 gives the sample of the stock quotation data. We give a pseudo name XYZ to our stock. In the left column of the table, we see items such as the Previous Close price, Open, Bid and Ask prices, Day's Price Range, 52 week Price Range, Volume, and Avg. Volume. In the right column, we have the listing of Market Cap (capitalization of the company), Beta, P/E ratio, Earning per share (EPS), Dividend & Yield, and Ex-dividend date. Here yield is the dividend amount divided by the stock price and expressed as a percentage. Beta in the table gives the correlation of the stock price variation with that of the corresponding Stock Index, such as S&P 500.

The value of beta equal to unity means full correlation between the variation of the company's stock price and that of the corresponding index. Beta less than 1 implies less variation and greater than 1 implies greater variation than that of the index. Ex-Dividend date is the terminal date after which the people buying the stock will not be eligible for the current dividend.

Table 3.1 Stock price data for the stock with symbol XYZ, say.

Previous Close	72.28	Market Cap	195.18B
Open	72.88	Beta	1.003
Bid	71.60 x 100	P/E Ratio	29.48
Ask	71.90 x 200	EPS	2.44
Day's Range	71.55 - 73.06	Earning Date	N/A
52wk Range	65.02 - 93.89	Dividend & Yield	2.65 (3.65%)
Volume	11,009,768	Ex-Dividend Date	N/A
Avg. Volume	10,064,700	1y Target Est	Not known

3.5 Company Profile

A brief description of the company is often available on the detailed quotation page or is accessed through a dropdown menu. It tells about the business in which the company is involved. It gives the segments it operates in, the details of the products that it makes and the markets in which it sells these products. It may tell about the number of facilities and where these are located. It may also tell about the competitor companies.

3.6 Other Valuation Measures

In addition to the valuation measures listed in section 3.3, the following measures are also relevant to the evaluation of stocks:

(a) Profitability

Profit Margin – It is the ratio of the total sales revenue minus the cost of goods and other expenses divided by the sales revenue and expressed as a percentage.

The higher the profit margin, the more profitable is the company.

(b) Valuation parameters – These parameters were covered in Section 3.3 and are as follows:

Price/ Earnings, Price/ Sales, Price/ Cash Flow

(c) Management Effectiveness

Return on assets – It is the ratio of the earnings divided by the assets of the company.

Return on equity – It is the ratio of the net income divided by stock holder equity.

Return on investments – It is the percentage return on an investment.

The greater the return on assets or equity, the more efficient is the operation of the company. In other words, the company is being managed more efficiently.

(d) Per Share Data
Earnings per share

Book value (BV) per share

Cash flow per share

Dividend per share

3.7 Enterprise Multiple

This valuation multiple is useful for valuing a company in case of takeover.

it is defined as the ratio of Enterprise Value to EBITDA and the ratio is known as the enterprise multiple. Here enterprise value equals the market value of equity plus debt minus cash. EBITDA is the abbreviation for the earnings before interest expenses, taxes, depreciation, and amortization. The ratio of enterprise value to EBITDA serves as proxy for how long it would take for an acquisition to earn enough to pay off its costs. The lower the value of this ratio, the better the company is from an investment perspective. Since enterprise multiples can vary depending upon the industry, they should be compared within the same industry.

3.8 Valuing Common Stocks by Price Multiples

In order to make money in the stock market, we need to be able to buy the shares of great companies at attractive prices. This requires that we estimate the price of stock based on the financial data available. The price multiples are fairly common for valuing stocks because they are easily available and are easy to apply. The following comments are relevant to the application of price multiples:

(a) The approach widely used by the investors for valuing common stocks makes use of the relationship between the price of stock (P), and the earnings per share (E), as given by the following equation

Price of stock = (P/E) × E

Multiplying the current P/E with the earnings per share estimate for the next year, we get the expected price of the stock for the next year. The uncertainty here is that the earnings estimates vary among the analysts and are often too optimistic. Another uncertainty is with the future P/E value which could be higher or lower than the current value. P/E depends upon a number of factors such as the type of business, product demand, sales and profit potential, pricing power, financial strength of the business and the economy in general. Simply speaking, P/E ratio reflects the investors' expectations about the future potential of the stock. The estimated future value of the stock would depend upon the future estimates of the P/E and the earnings/share.

While P/E is very common, it has problems because earnings can be boosted by accounting manipulations. Some consider P/S ratio as a better measure because sales are harder to manipulate as they have to be shown in the quarter they occur. However, there is problem if the company is showing large sales but is losing money with every transaction.

(b) The other multiples commonly used in valuing the stocks are P/S and P/B. These are calculated from the sales and book value information and their values are available on the financial websites. We compare each of these multiples for the company with the values in its own past, with those of the competitors, the industry index and the market averages such as S&P 500.

(©) For the growth stocks, we look at the PEG ratio instead of the P/B ratio. Note that such comparisons are not valid with the companies in different lines of businesses.

P/B ratio, which is the ratio of the stock price to the book value (shareholder equity or net worth) on the company balance sheet is relevant only for capital-intensive companies. These are the companies with large capital investment and inventory such as the automobile and agricultural equipment industries, rail road, steel mills, mining, etc. The P/B ratio is also useful for valuing financial services firms and banks because they have considerable liquid assets on their balance sheet. But the ratio is not useful for service firms.

The price-to-earnings growth ratio PEG is fairly popular for evaluating the growth companies. The companies with PEG ratio of one or less are considered fairly attractive for investment purposes.

3.9 Summary

1. The quantitative measures of stock valuation are P/E, PEG, P/B, P/S, P/CF, ROE, net profit margin, debt/equity ratio, etc.
2. The general financial strength of the company is indicated by the debt-to-equity ratio. The current ratio and the quick ratio indicate the ability of the company to pay for its current liabilities.
3. The basic stock quotation gives the Open, Bid and Ask prices, the

stock price range during the day as well as over the past 52 weeks, the volume of stock traded, market cap, earnings per share, PE ratio, and yield.

4. The financial data for a company can be retrieved from the financial websites. It is comprised of the items such as the valuation measures, financial highlights, management effectiveness, balance sheet items, income and cash flow, stock price history, share statistics, dividends and splits, etc.

Chapter 4

Financial Statements

4.1 Introduction

Stock market investing involves buying and selling the shares of a business- for-profit. In order to profit from this activity, the investor needs to understand in general how the business operates and what the finances of the company are. The latter can be done by looking at the financial documents of the company. These documents are issued by the company on a regular basis. These are known as the income statement, the balance sheet, and the cash flow statement. The fundamental stock valuation measures derive in large part from the financial data in these statements. Since the fundamental analysis involves mostly the valuation ratios, the expertise in accounting is not needed for this analysis.

4.2 Quarterly and Annual Reports

The companies listed on the stock exchanges are required to file quarterly and annual reports to the Securities and Exchange Commission (SEC) on a regular basis. The quarterly report, known as the 10-Q report, is filed every quarter except at the end of the fourth quarter when the annual report, known as the 10-K report, is filed which covers the entire year. These reports are available online from the EDGAR website (www.sec.gov/edgar.shtml) and also from the company website (http://www.pginvestor.com) under Annual Reports. The Annual Report describes what the company does and includes pictures of its products and employees. It starts with a letter from the Chief Executive Officer who provides an overall perspective of the company and its accomplishments over the past year. It is followed by the financial statements which provide important information related to the financial aspects of the company including the sales and profits. The companies prepare the annual

The companies prepare the annual report for dissemination at the annual meeting and to anyone on request. It is a good document to find out about the products , employees and financial aspects of the company. Following the recommendations of the investment banks and brokerage firms blindly is risky as learnt from the bankruptcies of Enron, WorldCom and others because of the conflict of interest. This stresses the need for individual analysis.

The annual 10-K report consists of four parts: business, financials, leadership, and other important information in fine print. It lists the management, the Board of Directors, and the items such as the executive compensation. The business section describes the core business, risks to the business, properties the company owns or leases, and the legal proceedings in which the company is involved. From the investment perspective, it is important to understand the business of the company. Unless we know how the company makes money, we will not be able to judge its suitability and desirability for investment. In the risk category, the companies list generally all the foreseeable risks to be on the safe side. One needs to pay attention only to the risks that may be important from the investment perspective. In the section on legal items, companies list all the ongoing legal cases and include comments how those could affect the company.

The financial section of the reports includes the financial statements which are the medium by which a company discloses information concerning its financial performance. These statements have the quantitative information which is used by the analysts to make investment decisions. The financial statements include the Income Statement, the Balance Sheet, and the Statement of Cash Flows. These were obtained here using the company website http://www.pginvestor.com under Annual Reports. These are also available on many finance websites such as http://finance.yahoo.com/ , http://www.nasdaq.com , http://annual reports.com and http://financials.morningstar.com/, etc. A handy source is your brokerage website which has the financial data, including these reports, from S&P Capital IQ.

In the analysis of stocks for investment by the investors, the income statement is the most important and so the details of it are given below. As for the other two statements, namely the Balance Sheet and the Cash Flow, the concepts are provided in this chapter but the details are given in the Appendix because they are mostly of interest to the analysts.

4.3 Income Statement

This statement tells us how the business is doing – what it is bringing in and what it is paying out. In other words, it provides an accounting of the revenues and the expenses of the company and the difference between the two amounts to net income or loss. The revenue comes from the sale of goods or services by the company. The company incurs different costs in producing this revenue. The first is the cost of materials, equipment, space, utilities, manpower etc. to produce the goods or to perform the services. The second is the cost associated with selling, general and administrative expenses. In addition to these costs, there may be capital expenditures related to the building, machinery and equipment.

Table 4.1 shows the income statement for Proctor and Gamble Co. for the years 2009 to 2011. The first row shows the total sales or revenue. This is basically the gross sales revenue minus any sales discounts and adjustment for returns, etc. The fact that the company has so much revenue does not mean that it is earning a profit. In order to determine the latter, we need to deduct the expenses of the business from the total revenues. These expenses are broken into various categories on the income statement. The first expense item is the cost of the products sold. This is the cost of the raw materials, labor and overhead in manufacturing the products. In the case of a general store such as Walmart, Target or Macys, it would be the cost of the goods purchased. For the service-related businesses, the cost of sales represents the cost of the services rendered. The difference between the net sales/ revenue and the cost of the products sold is the gross profit that is

Gross profit = total revenue – cost of revenue   (1)

From the sales revenue and the gross profit, the gross profit margin is calculated as below

Gross profit margin = Gross profit/ Sales revenue   (2)

By itself, the gross profit tells very little about the company but the gross profit margin tells a lot. It tells how well a company uses its production, purchasing and distribution resources to earn a profit. One should be on the lookout for downward trends in the gross profit margin over time because this could be a sign of future problems. When the cost of goods sold rises rapidly, the gross profit margin will be lower unless the company can pass these costs to the customers in the form of higher prices. Additionally, by comparing the gross profit margin ratios among various companies within the same industry, one can tell which company is more efficient.

The companies in the consumer goods such as food, general merchandise, automobiles etc. have high competition and so have limited pricing power. So their gross profit margins are low. The companies with durable economic advantage have higher gross profit margins which makes such companies desirable for long term investment. *So the gross profit margin could serve as a criterion in the initial selection of the company for investment.*

Next in the table are listed the interest expense and other non-operating expenses. The latter could include the expenses related to the research and development of new products, depreciation and amortization, restructuring and impairment charges, and the catch all "others" that includes all non- operating and non-recurring expenses. Subtracting the expenses from the net revenue or sales, and deducting the income taxes, we get the net earnings or loss. Knowing the number of shares of the company, we can calculate the earnings per share as shown.

The net earnings is used to calculate the earnings per share as follows

Earnings per share = net income/ number of shares of the company   (3)

The income statement gives the following items which are of interest in analyzing a company:

1. The total revenue (sales), listed as the first item in the table, is an important figure. For a growing company, the total revenue should be increasing year after year except in bad economic times such as the recession.
2. Operating income tells how profitable the company is. Comparing it over the years tells whether the profitability of the company is increasing or decreasing. For a progressive company the profitability should be expected to increase year after year.

Avoid looking at the income after tax because companies sometimes carryover losses resulting in irregular tax liability.

3. The interest expense should be fairly small in comparison to the sales or gross profit. This ensures that the company will not have any problem in making the interest payments on its debt which may be short term as well as long term.

4. The net income or earnings divided by the number of outstanding shares of the company gives the earnings per share (EPS) which is an important factor in the valuation of a company.

5. The stock price divided by the earnings per share gives the price- to-earnings (P/E) ratio. This ratio tells us what the investor is willing to pay for $1.00 earnings per share.

Table 4.1 Income Statement (Consolidated Statement of Earnings)

Amount in millions except per share amount, Years ended June 30

	2011	2010	2009
NET SALES	$82,559	$78,938	$76,694
Cost of products sold	40,768	37,919	38,690
Selling, general and administrative expense	25,973	24,998	22,630
OPERATING INCOME	15,818	16,021	15,374
Interest expense	831	946	1,358
Other non-operating income (expense), net	202	(28)	397
EARNINGS FROM CONTINUING OPERATIONS BEFORE INCOME TAXES	15,189	15,047	14,413
Income taxes on continuing operations	3,392	4,101	3,733
NET EARNINGS FROM CONTINUING OPERATIONS	11,797	10,946	10,680
NET EARNINGS FROM DISCONTINUED OPERATIONS	—	1,790	2,756
NET EARNINGS	$11,797	$12,736	$13,436
BASIC NET EARNINGS PER COMMON SHARE			
Earnings from continuing operations	$4.12	$3.70	$3.55
Earnings from discontinued operations	—	0.62	0.94
BASIC NET EARNINGS PER COMMON SHARE	4.12	4.32	4.49
DILUTED NET EARNINGS PER COMMON SHARE			
Earnings from continuing operations	3.95	3.53	3.39
Earnings from discontinued operations	—	0.58	0.87
DILUTED NET EARNINGS PER COMMON SHARE	3.93	4.11	4.26
DIVIDENDS PER COMMON SHARE	$1.97	$1.80	$1.64

Source: P&G Company website (http://www.pginvestor.com) under Annual Reports

6. The ratio of the net income divided by the total revenue of the company gives the profit margin.

From the income statement in Table 4.1, we get

Profit margin = $(11.797B/82,559)100 = 14.289$ %.

The income statement is also used to check the profitability of the company by using the following two ratios:

Operating margin = operating income/ gross profit or net sales   (4)

Net profit margin = earnings before taxes/ gross profit or net sale   (5)

The companies with high net profit margin have a big cushion in protecting themselves during a downturn while those with low profit margins can get wiped out.

In summary:

Gross profit equals the sales (booked but not necessarily paid) minus the direct cost ofproducing the company's product or service (which includes labor, material, and expenses directly attributable to producing it).

Operating income equals gross profit minus the expenses such as research, development, marketing, administrative etc.

    Net income equals the operating plus other income minus the interest and tax expenses.

The understanding of the income statement is essential in the analysis of the profitability and future growth of a company, as these are the major factors in deciding whether or not to invest in the company. Increasing sales (revenues) with consistency reflect strong fundamentals while rising margins indicate increasing efficiency and profitability. As for the profit fundamentals, look for the significant changes in revenues, cost of goods sold and the selling, general and administrative expenses.

4.4 Balance Sheet

It is the statement of the financial condition of the company at a particular date unlike the income statement which was for a particular quarter or year. Traditionally the accounting department creates the balance sheet at the end of each fiscal quarter. The balance sheet is based on the simple concept: what we have is the asset and what we have to pay is our liability, and the difference between the two is the equity. Suppose that we have $1000 in the bank account, so this is our asset money. If we have $600 in bills to pay, this is our liability. After the payment of our bills, we would be left with $1000 - $600 = $400. The leftover amount of $400 is our equity. In the balance sheet format, this would be stated as in Table 4.2.

Table 4.2 Format of Balance Sheet

Assets	
Cash in bank	$1000
Liabilities	
Payment of bills	$600
Equity	
Cash	$400

The same principle applies to the balance sheet of a company, the only difference being that its assets and liabilities are more diversified. With that as the background, we examine the Balance Sheet of Proctor & Gamble Co. given in Table 1 in the Appendix.

In the category of assets, the company has two types of assets: current assets and long-term assets. The current assets include the cash, short term investments (such as a short-term CD, 3 month treasuries, etc.), net receivables (payments expected for the sales already made), inventory, prepaid expenses and other assets (a sort of general slush fund). Prepaid expenses refer to the payments already made by the company to the vendor for the goods and services not yet received. The current assets are also sometimes referred to as the quick, liquid or floating assets. For the company, the total current assets at the end of June 30, 2011 are $21.97B (see Table 4.3). Note that the current assets are basically the working assets of the business because they are in the cycle of cash going to contribute to the inventory. The inventory is sold to vendors and becomes accounts receivable which when collected from the vendors turn back into cash. This cycle repeats itself over and over again and it is how a business makes money.

The long-term assets are those that have the holding period of more than one year. These include the following categories:

1. The investment in stocks, bonds and real estate recorded under long term investments.

2. The land, buildings, plant and equipment, etc. recorded at cost while accounting for depreciation. In some industries,such as the equipment and the automobile companies, the plant and equipment costs are significant because of the need for frequent replacement equipment costs are significant because of the need for frequent replacement..

In addition to the above, there are other assets as well. For example, when a company buys another company by paying a price in excess of the book value, the difference is recorded as the goodwill on the balance sheet. There are intangible assets which refer to the patents, copyrights, trademarks, franchises, brand name and the like. In the case of Proctor & Gamble Co. the intangibles refer to the brand name recognition and the proprietary processes used to produce the goods. Note that the companies are often acquired because of their proprietary technical knowhow and so the intangibles play an important role in arriving at the purchase price of the company.

Table 1. Balance Sheet for Proctor and Gamble Co. (PG)

Assets in millions June 30	2011	2010
CURRENT ASSETS		
Cash and cash equivalents	$ 2,768	$ 2,879
Accounts receivable	6,275	5,335
INVENTORIES		
Materials and supplies	2,153	1,692
Work in process	717	604
Finished goods	4,509	4,088
Total inventories	7,379	6,384
Deferred income taxes	1,140	990
Prepaid expenses and other current assets	4,408	3,194
TOTAL CURRENT ASSETS	21,970	18,782
PROPERTY, PLANT AND EQUIPMENT		
Buildings	7,753	6,868
Machinery and equipment	32,820	29,294
	934	850
Total property, plant and equipment	41,507	37,012
Accumulated depreciation	(20,214)	(17,768)
NET PROPERTY, PLANT AND EQUIPMENT	21,293	19,244
GOODWILL AND OTHER INTANGIBLE ASSETS		
Goodwill	57,562	54,012
Trademarks and other intangible assets, net	32,620	31,636
NET GOODWILL AND OTHER INTANGIBLE ASSETS	90,182	85,648
OTHER NONCURRENT ASSETS	4,909	4,498
TOTAL ASSETS	$138,354	$128,172

LIABILITIES AND SHAREHOLDERS' EQUITY

CURRENT LIABILITIES		
Accounts payable	8,022	7,251
Accrued and other liabilities	9,290	8,559
Debt due within one year	9,981	8,472
TOTAL CURRENT LIABILITIES	27,293	24,282
LONG-TERM DEBT	22,033	21,360
DEFERRED INCOME TAXES	11,070	10,902
OTHER NONCURRENT LIABILITIES	9,957	10,189
TOTAL LIABILITIES	70,353	66,733
SHAREHOLDERS' EQUITY		
Convertible Class A preferred stock	1,234	1,277
Common stock, stated value $1 per share	4,008	4,008
Additional paid-in capital	62,405	61,697
Reserve for ESOP debt retirement	(1,357)	(1,350)
Accumulated other comprehensive income (loss)	(2,054)	(7,822)
Treasury stock, at cost	(67,278)	(61,309)
Retained earnings	70,682	64,614
Non-controlling interest	361	324
TOTAL SHAREHOLDERS' EQUITY	68,001	61,439
TOTAL LIABILITIES AND SHAREHOLDERS' EQUITY	$138,354	$128,172

Source: P&G Company website (http://www.pgubvestor.com) under Annual Reports

The "other assets" include the assets that did not get counted in the above categories, for example the prepaid expenses or the tax recoveries to be received in future. The current assets added to the long-term assets give the total assets which for the Proctor and Gamble Co. were 138.354B in June 2011. The ratio of the net earnings to the total assets is known as the **asset ratio**. The higher the asset ratio, the more efficient is the company.

Similar to the assets, the liabilities of the company are also listed under the current and non-current categories. The liabilities refer to the payments that the company is obligated to make. The accounts payable refer to the money owed to the suppliers that have provided goods and services to the company on credit. Sometimes there are accrued expenses which are the liabilities that the company has incurred but has yet to be invoiced for. The long-term debt is the debt that matures after a year. "Other liabilities" is a catchall category in which the businesses pool their miscellaneous debts. The details of the major items in this category are included in the footnotes of the Balance Sheet. The deferred long term liability charges include the items such as the deferred income tax (tax that is due but has not been paid) and other such charges that have been deferred for payment. The current liabilities of the company are \$27.293B and the total liabilities are \$70.353B for the particular quarter end.

At the bottom of the table are the items contributing to the shareholder equity. It is accounted for under the headings of the preferred and common stocks, retained earnings, capital surplus etc. as listed in the table. The company's net earnings may either be paid out as dividends, used to buy back the company's shares or retained for future investment in the business. When they are retained, they appear on the balance sheet under shareholders' equity as retained earnings. If used profitably, they can greatly improve the profit picture of the company.

The shareholder equity tells about the stake of the shareholders in the business. From this we get the return on shareholder equity defined as follows:

Return on shareholder equity = Net earnings/ shareholder equity   (6)

The higher the return on shareholder's equity, the more profitable is the business for shareholders. This comparison is valid only for the companies in the same line of business.

From the stockholder equity, we calculate

Book value per share = Stockholder equity/ Number of shares

outstanding   (7)

Related to the balance sheet, the following questions are important in evaluating a company:

1. Is the company financially sound?

This is judged from the current ratio defined as follows:

Current ratio = current assets/ current liabilities   (8)

The higher the current ratio, the more liquid is the company. A current ratio of over one is considered good. For the companies with strong earnings power, the current ratio of less than one is also acceptable.

2. Are the amounts receivable reasonable?

These need to be watched because the company counts the sale as revenue as soon as the items are shipped. However, the company has yet to receive the payment from its vendors. If the vendors run in trouble financially, these payments may be in jeopardy. The receivable amount should be judged relative to the sales amount because the larger the sales, the greater will be the receivables. Considering that the total revenue from the sales in Table 4.1 was $82.559B in June 2011, the receivable amount of $6.275B in the corresponding quarter (Table 4.3) is not out of line.

3. Are the inventories at reasonable levels?

An abnormal increase in inventories could signal that the goods are not selling at the rate the company is producing them. This could spell trouble later. The inventories should be small in proportion to the sales and this needs to be examined with reference to the sales data.

4.5 Cash Flow Statement

The cash flow statement shows how much cash comes in and goes out of the company over the quarter or the year depending upon the quarterly or yearly report. It strips away all the non-cash items and tells how much cash the company actually generated. Considering that the companies produce and consume cash in operating, investing and financing activities, the cash flow statement is divided into the following three sections:

1. Cash flow from operating activities
2. Cash flow from investing activities
3. Cash flow from financing activities

The Cash Flow Statement for Proctor & Gamble Co. is given in Table 4.4 below. . It consists of the above three sections. The first line gives the net income of $11.797B for June 2011 which comes from the Income Statement (Table 4. 1). Listed below are the cash flows related to the operating activities. Adding these amounts to the net income, we get the total cash flow from operating activities as $13.231B. *Note that a company may have negative earnings and still have positive cashflow.*

In the next section, the cash flow from investing activities is listed. These activities involve capital expenditures, cash investments and other cash flows from investing activities. The capital expenditure is shown negative because it is the amount spent. The investments are positive because they add to the capital with the company. The total cash flows from investing activities may be positive or negative, it is -$3.482B here because of the large capital expenditures. Capital expenditure requirements may be huge in some industries such as the automobile, aerospace, appliances and other heavy equipment companies because of the need to replace heavy machinery due to wear and tear as well as the need for modernization. Since capital improvements last for years, they should be viewed in the time frame of 5-7 years. The companies requiring unusually large capital expenditures on a consistent basis need financing that eats into the profits. As a rough guideline, the capital expenditures should not exceed 50% of the annual net earnings of the company.

The third section lists the cash flows related to the financing activities of the company. The company is paying dividends and so the amount included is negative. The statement shows that the company is spending $7039B on buying back its shares. This amount is shown as negative. The shareholder friendly companies have share buyback policies. Since this activity reduces the number of outstanding shares, it has a positive effect on the earnings per share. If we add the numbers in various categories with proper signs, we end up with the total cash flows from financing activities in the amount of - $10.023B, as shown in the statement.

A key cash flow is the cash flow from operating activities. It is a key indicator of the financial strength of the company because, without the ability to generate cash flows from its operations, the company may not be able to survive. In order to keep growing at the present rate, the company needs capital expenditures. This brings in the concept of free cash flow which equals the cash flow from operating activities minus the capital expenditures.

Table 2 Consolidated Statements of Cash Flow

Amount in millions, Years ended June 30	2011	2010	2009
CASH AND CASH EQUIVALENTS	$ 2,879	$ 4,781	$ 3,313
OPERATING ACTIVITIES			
Net earnings	11,797	12,736	13,436
Depreciation and amortization	2,838	3,108	3,082
Share-based compensation expense	414	453	516
Deferred income taxes	128	36	596
Gain on sale of businesses	(203)	(2,670)	(2,377)
Change in accounts receivable	(426)	(14)	415
Change in inventories	(501)	86	721
Change in accounts payable, accrued and other liabilities	358	2,446	(742)
Change in other operating assets and liabilities	(1,190)	(305)	(758)
Other	16	196	30
TOTAL OPERATING ACTIVITIES	13,231	16,072	14,919
INVESTING ACTIVITIES			
Capital expenditures	(3,306)	(3,067)	(3,238)
Proceeds from asset sales	225	3,068	1,087
Acquisitions, net of cash acquired	(474)	(425)	(368)
Change in investments	73	(173)	166
TOTAL INVESTING ACTIVITIES	(3,482)	(597)	(2,353)
FINANCING ACTIVITIES			
Dividends to shareholders	(5,767)	(5,458)	(5,044)
Change in short-term debt	151	(1,798)	(2,420)
Additions to long-term debt	1,536	3,830	4,926
Reductions of long-term debt	(206)	(8,546)	(2,587)
Treasury stock purchases	(7,039)	(6,004)	(6,370)
Impact of stock options and other	1,302	721	681
TOTAL FINANCING ACTIVITIES	(10,023)	(17,255)	(10,814)
EFFECT OF EXCHANGE RATE CHANGES ON CASH AND CASH EQUIVALENTS	163	(122)	(284)
CHANGE IN CASH AND CASH EQUIVALENTS	(111)	(1,902)	1,468
CASH AND CASH EQUIVALENTS, END OF YEAR	$ 2,768	$ 2,879	$ 4,781

Source: P&G Company website (http://www.pginvestor.com) under Annual Reports

From the investment consideration, the following items deserve attention in the cash flow statement:

1. A decent cash flow (better yet free cash flow) from operating activities is very important because it enables the company to take care of capital expenditures, pay dividends and buy back its shares thereby benefitting the shareholders.

2. The capital expenditure needs of the company viewed over a time frame of 5-7 years should be moderate.

3. One needs to be on the lookout for write-offs in the cash flow statement which are supposedly a one-time charge. These could be labeled as the items such as "charges for reorganization of business" or "one-time charge for strategic actions." These could be for store closings or inventory write- downs. The write-offs indicate operating problems for the company.

4.6 Summary

1. The requirement for the companies listed on the stock exchanges is to file the quarterly reports (10-Q) and the annual report (10-K) every year. These can be accessed from the company or the Edgar website.
2. The financial section of the reports deals with the financial statements which are comprised of the Income Statement, the Balance Sheet, and the Statement of Cash Flows.
3. The revenue earned by the company comes from the Income Statement. The increase in revenue from year to year is an important indicator of the growth of the company.
4. The income statement gives the gross profit, operating expenses, operating income or loss, income from continuing operations, and the net income applicable to common shares. The net income divided by the number of outstanding shares of the company gives the earnings per share (EPS). The ratio of the net income divided by the total revenue of the company gives the profit margin. These are important parameters in the analysis of the company for investment.

5. The balance sheet provides listing of the current assets, long term investments, current and long term liabilities and stockholders' equity.

6. The asset ratio, defined as the ratio of the net earnings to the total assets, is an indicator of the efficiency of the company.

7. The ratio of the net earnings to the shareholder equity gives the return on shareholder equity. The higher the return on shareholder equity, the more profitable is the business for shareholders.

8. The current ratio defined as the ratio of the current assets to the current liabilities is an indicator of the financial strength of the company.

9. The cash flow statement shows the flow of cash in the operating, investing and financing activities of the company. It provides information about the free cash flow which provides flexibility to the company in its operations.

10. Look for consistency when looking at the financial statements. For example, does the company have consistent earnings, consistent growth in earnings, consistently high gross margins, etc.? A glitch here and there is acceptable.

11. Look at the capital needs of the business? If they are consistently high, that could be a problem.

12. The companies with high gross profit margin are better for investment.

Chapter 5

Selection and Analysis of Stocks for Investment

5.1 Introduction

Investing requires both the selection of stocks and their analysis for investment. Hence the chapter starts with the discussion of the considerations in the selection of stocks for investment. Of the many factors, it takes into account the industry classification and then considers the suitability of the business for investment in the context of the prevailing environment. It then considers the attributes of the particular company which leads to the decision if it is suitable for investment. This is followed by the discussion of the steps in the analysis of the particular company for investment.

5.2 Basic Consideration in the Selection of a Company for Investment

When considering to invest in the stock market, the question is which stock to buy. As a matter of principle, one should not consider buying the stock of a company that one does not understand. The questions to ask in this context are:

1. To what industry does the company belong?
2. What does the company do and what are its products?
3. What is the demand for the products of the company?
4. How established is the company business?
5. How does the company make money?

Regarding question 1, it should be recognized that there are a large number of industries to which the company may belong. One industry classification, as used by the financial publication Value Line Investment Survey, is given in Table 5.1.

Table 5.1 Industry classification by Value Line Investment Survey.

Aerospace/Defense	Metal fabricating
Air transport	Reinsurance
Automotive	Retail automotive
Auto parts	Petroleum (producing)
Cable TV	Office equipment and supplies
Chemical (basic and diversified)	Oilfield services and equipment
Diversified companies	Packaging and container
Electric utility	Petroleum (integrated)
Engineering and construction	Pharmacy services
Entertainment	Publishing
Hotel/Gaming	Recreation
Rail road	Restaurant
Heavy truck and equipment	Retail store
Telecom utility	Retail/wholesale food
Trucking	Telecom services
Medical services	Tobacco

Note that in every classification there are a large number of businesses. For example, in the first category 'Aerospace/Defense' there are a large number of companies dealing with both the civilian and defense items. The following is the list often major companies in the aerospace and defense sectors:

United Technologies (UTX) - in everything from elevators and escalators to helicopters and fuel cell systems.

Boeing (BA) - in the development and manufacture of civil and military aircrafts, helicopters and space missile systems.

Lockheed Martin (LMT) - in space, telecommunications, electronics, and aeronautics systems.

General Dynamics (GD) - in combat vehicles, weapons systems and munitions, and shipbuilding.

Northrop Grumman (NOC) - in aerospace, electronics, information systems and shipbuilding.

Raytheon (RTN) - in mission systems integration for communications and intelligence systems as well as mission support services.

Goodrich (GR) - in passenger restraint systems, pump and engine control, de- icing systems and aircraft evacuation systems.

Rockwell Collins (COL) - in communications and avionics and in-flight entertainment systems.

L-3 Communication Holdings (LLL) – in command control, communications, intelligence and surveillance and reconnaissance systems.

With reference to question 2, we need to know what particular items the company produces and in question 3 what is the demand of the items being produced by the company. This is important from the consideration of investment because the company dealing with defense equipment will be expected to do well when the defense budget is on the rise. As for the Boeing Co. which has a major part of its business in the manufacture of civilian planes, the important consideration is the backlog which deals with the orders of planes already placed but are yet to be supplied by the company. This takes us to question 3 above because backlog indicates the demand.

Referring to question 4, all the companies listed above are well established and have moats of their own which refers to entry barriers by other companies. It should be noted that question 4 is more important for a small company which may be trying to establish itself. Lastly question 5 refers to how the company makes money. This relates to the operation of the company involving items such as the cost of production, pricing, profit margin, capital investment, financing, research and development etc.

5.3 Economic Considerations in the Selection

of a Company for Investment

For the stock of a company to do well, the basic requirement is that the company does well in terms of the profits. Along with other factors, the latter are affected by the economy and the monetary policy (For detailed discussion see Chapter 14). For example, in a recessionary environment, the public is squeezed financially. It still has to buy the items of necessities such as food, general hygiene, medicines and clothing. One would thus expect the companies dealing with such items to do well. The examples of such companies are Kraft Foods, Kroger, Safeway, Whole Foods Market, etc. in the category of food; Colgate Palmolive and Proctor & Gamble in the category of general hygiene; Abbott Labs, Pfizer, Johnson and Johnson and Medtronic in the category of pharmaceutical and medical services; and Walmart, Target, Dollar General, Family Dollar Stores etc. for the general needs of daily use. If the economy is picking up, the demand would be expected to increase in the industries such as construction, restaurant, entertainment, transport, railroad, etc. In a thriving economy, the demand in the industries such as air travel, recreation, luxury goods, automobiles, restaurant, hotels and casinos etc. will be high.

In the case of accommodative monetary policy, the interest rates are low. Such an environment leads to the greater demand for housing and housing- related items such as lumber, roofing, insulation, flooring, cabinetry, bathroom fixtures, kitchen appliances, heating and cooling equipment, paints and electrical furnishings. The new homes need kitchen and laundry appliances, furniture and landscaping materials, etc. In the low interest rate and high employment environment, the affordability is increased. This leads to greater demand for cars and other discretionary items.

As the knowledge of the sectors and industries for investment is important, a separate chapter 7 dealing with the related aspects is included to help the readers expand their choices for investment.

5.4 Attributes of a Company for Investment

Investing in the stock market requires buying the shares of a business with the expectation that it will grow with time resulting in increased profit. In

other words, the business will become worth more and so the share price will increase. The return on investment would depend on how well the business does. So the key to making money in the stock market is finding companies which have good appreciation potential with as little risk as possible. The prerequisites for this potential in the company are described below:

1. The company has a moat which means that its products and services are not easily duplicated.
2. The company is in a business whose products are in demand. If there is no market for its goods or services, there is no chance for its growth or the pricing power.
3. The company has an edge over other companies in the same line of business. This could be in various forms depending upon the business. Some of these are the lead-in product introduction, product quality, cost advantage, brand recognition, reliability, and service after sales, etc.
4. The company has a plan for the improvement of its products and sustained profitability. If it is a growth company, it has the proven record of the growth of earnings on a consistent basis. If it is a value company, it has the plan to increase earnings by opening more stores, streamlining operations or restructuring.
5. The company has free cash flow to sustain its operations, develop new products and support growth.
6. The company has high profit margin and a good return on its investment.
7. The company is financially sound to support the operation and expansion of its business.
8. The company has competent management with the proven record of accomplishment.
9. The stock of the company is reasonably priced based on its past history, other businesses in its sector and the broad market.

5.5 Companies to Avoid for Investment

The list of the companies that may be considered for investment is vast. It would thus be prudent to narrow down the list by applying the followingother words, the business will become worth more and so the share price willincrease. The return on investment would depend on how well the business does.So the key to making money in the stock market is finding companies which have good appreciation potential with as little risk as possible. The prerequisites for this potential in the company are described below:

1. The company has a moat which means that its products and services are not easily duplicated.
2. The company is in a business whose products are in demand. If there is no market for its goods or services, there is no chance for its growth or the pricing power.
3. The company has an edge over other companies in the same line of business. This could be in various forms depending upon the business. Some of these are the lead-in product introduction, product quality, cost advantage, brand recognition, reliability, and service after sales, etc.
4. The company has a plan for the improvement of its products and sustained profitability. If it is a growth company, it has the proven record of the growth of earnings on a consistent basis. If it is a value company, it has the plan to increase earnings by opening more stores, streamlining operations or restructuring.
5. The company has free cash flow to sustain its operations, develop new products and support growth.
6. The company has high profit margin and a good return on its investment.
7. The company is financially sound to support the operation and expansion of its business.
8. The company has competent management with the proven record of accomplishment.
9. The stock of the company is reasonably priced based on its past history, other businesses in its sector and the broad market.

5.5 Companies to Avoid for Investment

The list of the companies that may be considered for investment is vast. It would thus be prudent to narrow down the list by applying the following

criteria as the basis for exclusion:

1. Avoid the companies with very small capitalization and those that trade on the bulletin boards or pink sheets.
2. Avoid initial public offerings (IPOs), particularly those that have no track record of profitability. These are often timed to benefit the entrepreneurs at the expense of new stockholders.
3. Avoid the companies which claim to have developed a unique product while still losing money. There is too much uncertainty here as regards to the acceptability of the product and profit potential considering that a large percentage of such enterprises fail.
4. Avoid the companies that do not generate cash flow from the operating activities on a sustained basis. This is so because the cash flow is needed to develop new products and services which are needed for growth.

5.6 Steps in the Analysis of a Company for Investment

1. Look at the business profile of the company which is available at your broker's website. Assess the potential for growth and profitability of the company in view of its products and the current economic environment.
2. Examine the trading particulars of the company from the quotation obtained from your broker's website. Pay attention to the following valuation measures:

Price to earnings ratio (PE) Price
to sales ratio

Price to book ratio or Price to cash flow ratio PEG
(P/E to growth ratio)
Dividend yield

3. Check for the growth.

Revenues, Gross profit and/or Net Income (or Earnings per share) in the Income Statement available on your broker's website

4. Check for the profitability in terms of the Gross Margin and Operating Margin from Statistics on the Yahoo Finance website or Brokerage website.
5. Check for the management effectiveness from the following:

Return on Equity and Return on Assets in Profitability under Statistics on Yahoo Finance website

6. Check for the free cash flow on the Brokerage website or in the Statistics on Yahoo Finance website
7. Check for the financial health in terms of the following: Current ratio, Buildup of inventories, Receivables etc.

5.7 Analysis of Stocks Using the Internet Brokerage Website

The brokerages have lately expanded their websites to provide the relevant data accessible to their clients so that they can directly select stocks for investment. In addition to that, there are reports available from investment research firms which clients can access as well.

As already mentioned in Chapter 2, in order to buy stocks, an investor needs a brokerage account which can be opened by satisfying the minimum amount requirement. Appendix 2.1 provides a list of the brokerages. The investor places the order to buy or sell the securities in this account. We will use Charles Schwab brokerage (www.client.Schwab.com) as an example because I have access only to this site because of my account there. The same treatment should apply to other brokerages as well. This brokerage offers commission-free trading to its clients. Many other internet brokerage companies are also doing the same.

When you sign in the brokerage site to access your account, it leads directly to the screen giving Research\Stocks\ Overview\Schwab Stock Lists\ Charts\Screeners etc. Schwab provides its own list of A-rated stocks and the stocks of the ratings lower than A. In addition to that it provides other lists of stocks as well using the criteria such as outperformers, global companies, large cap stocks, mid cap stocks, etc. You may pick any stock from this list or outside the list for your analysis and collect the relevant data. The outline of the steps and the analysis of stocks is presented below using the data from Schwab Brokerage internet site.

5.8 Outline for Stock Analysis

Company Name

Recommendation BUY / NOT BUY   Price ------

Trailing 12 month EPS

Market Capitalization

Trailing 12 month P/E   Yield %

Look at Price Performance Plot – as a function of the time for 1 day, 5 day, 1 month to 5 years if needed

News related to the business aspects of the company

Annual dividend rate and yield

Earnings (estimate and actual) for different quarters

Revenue for the same four quarters as above Price

to Earnings ratio (PE)

Price to Earnings Growth ratio (PEG) if available

Highlights: Sales forecast, Operating margin forecast etc,

Investment Rationale/Risk – Buy or Not Buy

Revenue per share data - yearly for a few years

Earnings per Share data - yearly for a few years

Dividend Data

The above is supplemented with reports from the evaluation companies. Some of these companies are **Morningstar, Refinitiv, CFRA and Market Edge..**

From the above it is seen that virtually all the information needed for decision to reach whether the stock is fit to invest at this price level or not is available, Prior to the internet, it took a lot of effort and time to assemble this kind of data to arrive at any conclusion.

5.9 Stock Analysis Examples Using Charles Schwab Brokerage

(a) Company name - Mastercard (Symbol MA)

Mastercard Inc

MA
NYSE

Outperform

ESG RATING

Environmental, Social, and Governance (ESG) Ratings Overview

MSCI ESG Rating

Laggard	Average	Leader

Weighted Average Key Issues Score — Leader

Environmental — Leader

Social — Average

Governance — Average

OTHER OPINIONS

CFRA

Recommendation

Morningstar Rating

Argus 12 Month Rating

Market Edge Second Opinion®

Reuter's Average Rating

EARNINGS PER SHARE

Fiscal Year ending in December

vs. prior year (%)

Earnings Surprise (%)

# of analysts

REVENUE

Fiscal Year ending in December

vs. 1 year ago (%)

ANNUAL EARNINGS FORECAST

12/31/2024	$14.37		$14.10 - $14.85	37
12/31/2025	$16.67	$0.00	$16.90 - $17.73	37
Next 5 Yr. Growth Rate	19.2%	0.0%	15.8% - 20.8%	3

DIVIDENDS

Dividends are paid on a Quarterly basis.

BUSINESS DESCRIPTION

Mastercard Incorporated is a technology company that connects consumers, financial institutions, merchants, governments and businesses across the world, enabling them to use electronic forms of payment. It allows users to make payments by creating a range of payment solutions and services using its brands MasterCard, Maestro and Cirrus. It enables a variety of payment capabilities (including products and value-added services and solutions) over its multi-rail networks among account holders, merchants, financial institutions, businesses, governments and others, offering customers and partners for their payment needs. Its products include consumer credit, consumer debit, prepaid, B2B accounts payable, commercial point of sale, disbursements and remittances, and others. It offers additional payment capabilities that include automated clearing house (ACH) transactions (both batch and real-time account-based payments). It also offers other services, such as cyber and intelligence solutions.

Profile - It is a technology company which provides transaction processing and other payment related products and services in the USA and internationally. It was selected because it is probably the most well-known business in the present economy of paying for every purchase using credit card.

The price of the stock on the day of analysis August 15, 2024 was $468.71. It showed the plot showing the variation of stock price with time during the day as well as over varying periods from day 1 to 5 years by clicking to these time periods. It is not being shown here because it is the first item that shows when you enter the stock name for quotation. It was followed by the news about the stock.

For the analysis of the stock, we click at the Schwab Equity Ratings Report on the right side of the Schwab quotation screen. It can be accessed directly from Charles Schwab quotation page and is shown here as a sample. Note that it gives the description of the business. In addition to that it gives the earnings per share for the years 2020 to 2023 as well as the earnings estimate by 31 analysts for the year 2024. It is $14.31 for the year 2024. Below that is the revenue comparison of 27.948 B. In addition to this, there is earnings estimate comparison with the previous quarters as well as the last four years. It should be noted that the earnings estimate for the year 2024 is $14.31 per share compared to $11.83 for the year 2023 which is excellent. The revenue estimate for the year 2024 is $27.94 B versus $25.10 B in the year 2023 which is good. The next 5-year growth rate is expected to be 19.2% which also good. The dividend per share also increased from $1.96 in the year 2022 to $2.28 in the year 2023. The whole picture is thus positive for investment in the stock.

Charles Schwab provided Outperform rating to this stock which was also supported by other rating agencies such as CFRA which gave it 4* and Argus which gave BUY rating, as seen on the top right corner of the Schwab Equity Ratings Report. You can access these reports from Charles Schwab Brokerage site as well. For more analysis, you may refer to the detailed report by CFRA which can also be accessed from Charles Schwab Brokerage website. It provides detailed discussion of the stock, its justification for the current rating and expected stock prices along with the appreciation potential and tabular comparison of the revenues and profits for the next four quarters.

It is not being produced here because of the copyright restriction.

It is not being produced here because of the copyright restriction.

(b) Company name – Amazon

Profile - Amazon.com, Inc. engages in the retail sale of consumer products, advertising and subscriptions service through online and physical stores. The company operates through three segments: North America, International, and Amazon Web Services (AWS). It manufactures and sells electronic devices, including Kindle, Fire tablets, Fire TVs, Echo, Ring, Blink, etc. It offers programs that enable sellers to sell their products in its stores; and programs that allow authors, independent publishers, musicians, filmmakers, skill and app developers and others to publish and sell content. Furthermore, it provides compute, storage, database, analytics, machine learning as well as advertising services through programs, such as sponsored ads, display, and video advertising. It serves consumers, sellers, developers, enterprises, content creators, advertisers and employees.

Price on August 16, 2024 $177.04

Current P/E on Operating EPS 2024E = 28.77

For the analysis, we look at the Schwab Equity Ratings Report which can be accessed from the quotation screen, as indicated in the previous example. It gives it the Outperform rating. On the right side, we have all kinds of data related to the value, growth, momentum and financial matrices. On the other side of the page, it gives the annual earnings forecast per share which is $4.73 for the year 2024 and $5.82 for the next year. The other rating agencies namely CFRA and Morningstar give it the rating of 4 stars and Argus simply gives BUY rating. For more analysis, you may refer to the detailed report by CFRA which can also be accessed from Charles Schwab Brokerage website. It provides the detailed discussion about the stock along with the revenue and expected profits as well as the full justification for its rating.

(©) Company name -- Meta Platforms (Symbol META)

Profile - Meta Platforms

It engages in the development of products that enable people to connect with others through mobile devices, personal computers and virtual reality headsets. It operates in two segments, Family of Apps and Reality Labs. The Family of Apps segment offers Facebook, which enables people to share and connect   with interests; Instagram for sharing photos, videos and private messages; Messenger for people to connect with others and WhatsApp for people and businesses to communicate and transact privately. The Reality Labs segment provides augmented and virtual reality related products.

Price on August 16, 2024 $ 526.80

Earnings

Year 2024 $21.23 Year

2025 $24.08

Next 5 year growth rate 13.6%

Revenue

Year 2023 $134.90 B Year

2024 $161.63 B

The ratings by CFRA is 4* and 2* by Morningstar and BUY by Argus.

The total assets increased from $133,376 to 229,623 millions from the year 2019 to year 2023. For the same period the liabilities were from $15,053 to $31,960 millions. The company is thus in good financial condition.

It then gives the financial statements for the company in terms of the income statement, balance sheet and cash flow statements on the internet site. These were discussed in Chapter 4 of the book in terms of their relevance and so are not being repeated here. The revenue and the Earnings per share data is available in the CFRA Report on your brokerage website, as used in the above examples. They lead to the judgement for the suitability of the stock for investment and that is what we want in our analysis.

Finally, the choice is yours how you get the required information whether from the brokerage site, CRFA report or any other source. The important thing is that it is needed for the analysis of stocks.

5.10 Narrowing the List

It should be recognized that the number of companies is vast and so the investor needs to narrow down the selection. This may be done based on the specific criteria. For example, a person may like to consider investing in the hot areas which are popular in the 20th century such as internet, data, cloud, artificial intelligence, etc. It should be recognized that the stocks of such companies will be volatile but have the potential of greater return. Others may be interested in the companies related to climate change. Some may see a greater return from healthcare related companies. People in retirement may not be able to withstand the wild fluctuation in stock prices and so may be interested in dividend paying stocks with stable prices. Some brokers such as Fidelity provide the list of stocks based on such themes. The clients of Charles Schwab, Merrill Edge and Wells Trade have access to the lists of stocks selected by their advisors.

In order to help the readers, Chapter 7 in the book with the title "Sectors and Industries for Investment" covers the whole spectrum of industries along with their names and a brief description of their business. You will find many names that that are familiar to you and they can be the candidates for investment. However, keep in mind that you invest in a business that has the record and future potential to make increasing revenue and also the increasing profit year after year. For this you need to look at the past record and the future estimates of the analysts. The past records are available on the brokerage site and the analyst estimates on a site like Schwab Equity Ratings Report shown earlier as well as the CFRA Report which you can access from Schwab Brokerage site.

If you find the above overwhelming, look around and see which business is hot. The problem is that it keeps changing with time. For example, at one time Walmart was very popular for groceries but other businesses have caught up with it. However, it is still popular because it is all the time expanding in other areas such as data centers and artificial intelligence. When i-phones were introduced, they were very popular but many companies in China, Korea and other countries came up with competing models and their sales decreased and this affected the stock prices. Now the companies are trying to introduce artificial intelligence in these devices and the mere prospect of this is increasing the sales potential. The same thing applies to GOOLE which dominated in search engine and that is also being threatened now. Companies such as Dell and HP were very popular in the early days of computer introduction but their sales decreased when the market got saturated. They are catching up again because of the infusion of artificial intelligence in the computers.

The same thesis applies to the companies in the medical industry. In the Covid days Moderna and Pfizer were very popular for their vaccines. Eli Lilly and Novo Nordisk came up with the weight loss medicines and that wiped out the Weight Watchers business. Eli Lilly's new Alzheimer drug for the treatment of dementia has now been approved. It follows another drug Leqembi introduced by Eisai and Biogen.

The above description shows that the change with time is a normal process and so doing the very best in investing involves staying with the developments on evolving basis and capitalizing on them as and when they occur. This is not easy unless you keep up with the business news through newspapers and other business publications. In this respect I recommend Wall Street Journal and Barrons strongly. In Chapter 13 on Financial Resources many such publications have been described for your guidance.

If you do not have the time or inclination to go through the keep up with the ongoing developments in the business word, I suggest that you invest in the market indexes covered in Chapter 10 Table 10.2 such as SPY (Standard & Poor's 500), MDY (Standard & Poor's 400), QQQ (NASDQ 100) etc. For various market sectors, you may invest in the ETFs in Table 10.3. You invest in them just like individual stocks on the broker website. Another choice is to invest in mutual funds covered in Chapter 9 where the selection of the securities is made by a team of experts for the specific areas and monitored by them as well on an ongoing basis.

In any case, I do not advise investing in speculative stocks which are new and have no record of earnings. Many of those fail and you will have nothing but losses. Do not bet your hard-earned earnings on them. Instead invest in companies that you know and have a solid record of earnings and profits.

Suggested Action Items

Considering the present economic conditions, pick two growth stocks and two value stocks. Learn about the companies and study their financial data.

Analyze them for investment and pick the best one of each kind. Buy a few shares of the two companies selected in about the same amount and monitor them regularly for the price along with the related news. You are now an investor in the stock market. Try to find your comfort level with this experience.

Chapter 6

Technical Analysis of Stocks

6.1 Introduction

The evaluation of stocks presented in chapter 5 using the financial data utilizes the approach known as the Fundamental Analysis. In this chapter, an alternative approach known as the Technical Analysis is presented. This approach is based on the study of the charts showing the price and trading volume patterns of the stock. These patterns are used in the analysis of the momentum of stock and the support and the resistance levels. These are supplemented with some technical parameters in the investment decisions. The coverage of technical analysis here is very limited and is presented to introduce simple technical analysis principles as a supplement to the fundamental analysis.

6.2 Technical Analysis versus Fundamental Analysis

Unlike the fundamental analysis, which considers the financial data in evaluating a stock, the technical analysis uses charts to study the price movements along with trading volumes of the stock. In fact the technical analysis does not even look at the revenues and earnings data. The following are the basic tenets of the technical analysis:

1. The stock price and its movement up or down is the result of interaction between the supply and the demand.
2. The price of a stock moves in trends that persist for a long period of time. The reversal in the trend occurs as a result of the changes in

supply and demand. The changes in trends can be detected by analyzing the price movements along with trading volumes over a period of time. These trends can be spotted by careful analysis and used for the buy and the sell signals.

3. The chart patterns often repeat themselves.

Consistent with the above principles, technical analysts analyze daily, weekly and monthly fluctuations in the price of the stock in conjunction with the volume of stock traded and use the signals generated by the charts in trading decisions.

The decision to buy or sell securities based on the technical analysis alone is not recommended. For sound evaluation, the fundamental analysis must be considered. *It is suggested that a prudent investor use basically the fundamental analysis and look at the chart patterns to gage the direction of the stock or the market as a whole.* The fundamentals deal with items such as the revenue, earnings, profits, profit margin, etc. which tell how the company is doing. These are the factors that basically govern the stock price. The technical charts reveal whether the stock price is going up or down and with what kind of volume support. While these observations may be important, they should not be the sole basis for investment in the stock.

6.3 Technical Indicators

From the variation in the price of stock over time, a number of technical indicators may be derived. Some of these are the following:

Simple Moving Average (SMA)

Exponential Moving Average (EMA)

Moving Average Convergence Divergence (MACD)

Money Flow Index (MFI)

Relative Strength Index (RSI)

Bollinger Bands (BB)

Stochastic Oscillator

The plot of these technical indicators is facilitated using the technical chart period of time. These trends can be spotted by careful analysis and used for the buy and the sell signals.

4. The chart patterns often repeat themselves.

Consistent with the above principles, technical analysts analyze daily, weekly and monthly fluctuations in the price of the stock in conjunction with the volume of stock traded and use the signals generated by the charts in trading decisions.

The decision to buy or sell securities based on the technical analysis alone is not recommended. For sound evaluation, the fundamental analysis must be considered. *It is suggested that a prudent investor use basically the fundamental analysis and look at the chart patterns to gage the direction of the stock or the market as a whole.* The fundamentals deal with items such as the revenue, earnings, profits, profit margin, etc. which tell how the company is doing. These are the factors that basically govern the stock price. The technical charts reveal whether the stock price is going up or down and with what kind of volume support. While these observations may be important, they should not be the sole basis for investment in the stock.

6.3 Technical Indicators

From the variation in the price of stock over time, a number of technical indicators may be derived. Some of these are the following:

Simple Moving Average (SMA)

Exponential Moving Average (EMA)

Moving Average Convergence Divergence (MACD)

Money Flow Index (MFI)

Relative Strength Index (RSI)

Bollinger Bands (BB)

Stochastic Oscillator

The plot of these technical indicators is facilitated using the technical chart facility which is available on many financial websites. The website www.stockcharts.com provides this on a subscription basis. The yahoo finance website (http://finance.yahoo.com) provides free access to this facility for personal use. The free charting facility is available on most brokerage websites as well. On the chart diagram, there is a location marked 'Add Indicator' which when clicked opens the list of various technical indicators. Clicking on any particular indicator results in its plot on the diagram.

The typical chart for a stock is shown in Fig. 6.1. Of all the technical indicators, the most commonly used technical indicator is the moving average which is defined as the average of stock prices over the last number of days specified. Thus 50-day moving average line is obtained by connecting the points obtained by taking the average of closing stock prices over the last 50 days. Similarly the 200-day moving average line is obtained by taking the average of closing stock prices over the last 200 days. These lines are shown on the technical chart in Fig. 6.1. Notice that the moving averages smooth out the stock price fluctuation and hence show the general trend in the variation of the stock price with time. Other time intervals are also used for identifying the trends. The shorter the time interval, the more is the fluctuation in the moving average curve. Similar to the (simple) moving average lines, we can get the exponential moving average (EMA) line plots as well.

The interplay of the short term and the long term moving averages is commonly used as the indicator of the bearish or bullish signal. For example, when the 50-day moving average line on its way down crosses the 200-day moving average line, it is said to form a death cross which is a bearish signal. Conversely, when the 50-day moving average line climbs above the 200-day moving average line, it is said to form a golden cross which is considered to be a bullish signal. It has been reported that the data going back to year 1896 show that anytime the 50 -day moving average of the broad market index (such as SPY) is below the 200-day moving average, the probability of a down behavior is 36%, up substantially from the base probability of 18% in a normal course. Similar probability could be applied to the direction of the specific stock price movement as well.

It should be noted here that the technical analysis is not an exact science but it does serve as the probable indicator of the direction of the market or the price of stock.

6.4 Moving Average Convergence Divergence

Related to the moving averages is a technical parameter known as MACD. It is an abbreviation for "Moving Average Convergence Divergence" and is obtained by clicking on MACD in the 'Add Indicator ' location. Here 'CD ' stands for "convergence and divergence," and so MACD refers to the phenomenon of the short-term and long-term moving averages coming together and spreading apart. For MACD the short term moving average used is 12-days and the long term moving average is 26-days. During the period of strong stock price trend, the two moving average lines grow further apart (that is diverge) and during sideways consolidation in stock price they converge or come closer together, often crisscrossing one another. MACD thus depicts what can be seen from the divergence and convergence between the two moving average lines. The MACD plot is also shown in Fig. 6.1.

6.5 Market Momentum Indicators

Technical analysis is based on the concept that stocks with strong momentum in one direction or another are likely to stay in that direction for extended periods of time. So the success in investing depends upon the ability to recognize the change in the direction of the stock price and making use of it. The momentum has to do with investor psychology which certainly is an important element in stock market behavior. As the shares of a strong performer continue to climb in price, new investors jump aboard, hoping for the duplication in performance that preceded their buying. This pushes the stock price further up. Likewise, when a stock starts going down in price, more and more investors join in unloading the stock and so this action feeds in the frenzy of selling stock. This process continues until the stock gets oversold and new buyers jump in thereby changing the direction.

Technical analysts use many parameters for market momentum such as the Relative Strength Indicator (RSI), Money Flow Index (MFI), and Stochastic Oscillator. The parameter RSI compares the magnitude of recent gains to recent losses in an attempt to determine the overbought and the oversold conditions of the stock. It ranges from 0 to 100. The stock is considered to be overbought when RSI approaches the 80 level, meaning that it is getting overvalued and is likely to pull back. When RSI approaches the 20 level, it indicates that the stock is getting oversold and so is likely to rebound. We will see the plot of RSI on a chart in the next section.

Stochastic Oscillator is a technical momentum indicator obtained by comparing the stock's closing price to its price range over a given period of time. Money Flow Index (MFI) is a momentum indicator used to measure the amount of money flowing into and out of the stock.

6.6 Technical Analysis Applied to a Specific Stock

Figure 6.1 shows the typical technical chart for a stock, say XYZ. Note that the vertical axis represents the price of stock on the date represented by the horizontal axis. Thus the plot represents the closing prices on the particular dates. Since the stock price fluctuates daily, the curve representing the price of stock over time is zigzag in nature. Here the horizontal axis represents the period of one year, June 5, 2014 – June 4, 2015. The period can be changed by selecting the desired time period in the Range setting. The vertical lines on the time axis show the volume traded (in millions) on any particular day. On this diagram, the 50-day and 200-day moving average lines are also shown. These were obtained by selecting 50 and 200 Moving Avg. The lower plot on the diagram shows the MACD curve.

It should be noted from Fig. 6.1 that the stock price fluctuates almost daily. The price of the stock goes up or down depending upon the supply and demand imbalance caused by the incoming 'buy' and 'sell' trade orders which are affected by the assessment of the company on an ongoing time basis. If there is news about the earnings of the company being better than the analyst estimates and/or a brighter future outlook for the company business, the price of the stock should rise. Other positive news such as the discovery of a new product with perceived consumer appeal, favorable legislation, new contract award, large award from a legal settlement, etc. would also help to raise the price of the stock. On the other hand, if there is news about the revenue or earnings short-fall or some other negative development about the company, the stock price would be expected to go down. Technical analysts analyze the variation in stock price in conjunction with the volume of stock traded. Thus, according to them if the increase in the price of stock is large and is accompanied by a large increase in trading volume, it is bullish for the stock. Similarly the decrease in stock price accompanied by a large volume is bearish for the stock. The increase in stock price with the decrease in volume and vice versa is considered indecisive.

We now pay attention to the stock price variation in Fig. 6.1. Notice that the stock price shot up from point A accompanied by the sharp increase in volume. Technical Analysts take this as a bullish indicator raising the prospect of a **Buy** signal. Except for the minor daily fluctuations in price, the stock kept going up until point B. From B to C the stock price went down but was still above the 50-day moving average line. During this period, the volume traded was decreasing with time. This shows that the selling was on the decline which is positive for the stock. An investor need not be overly concerned with the decrease in stock price so long as it stays above the 50- day moving average line unless there is a sudden large drop in price accompanied by a large volume. In the latter case, the likelihood of some bad news affecting the price of stock should be expected and this needs close scrutiny by the investor and revaluation of the stock. Considering that the stocks never go up in a straight line, a behavior like this is expected. If the stock price dips below the 50-day moving average line, one should become cautious. In Fig. 6.1 this occurred at point D. One needs to see here if this is due to the routine fluctuation in stock price or due to some adverse development. In the latter case, the stock should be sold. Otherwise the stock should be closely monitored with the expectation of it going up again. This is what happened in the present case as the stock reversed its course and kept going up without touching the 50 day moving average line up to point E. After this the stock price dipped below the 50 day moving average line and the fall in stock price was accompanied by large increases in trading volumes. The stock should have been sold close to point E.

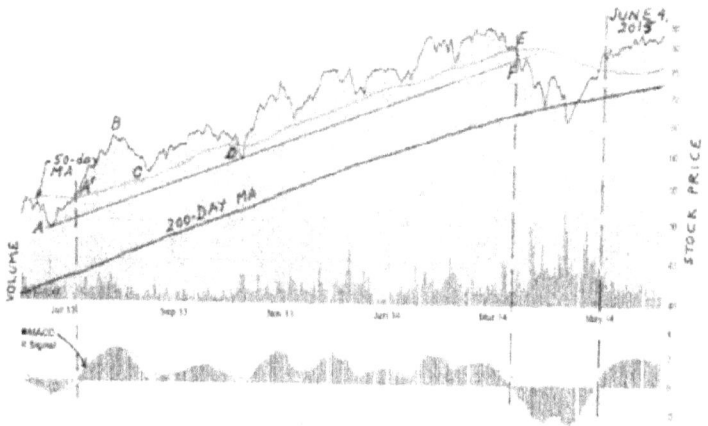

Figure 6.1 Technical chart showing the price variation and trading volume for XYZ stock over a period of one year, with 50-day and 200-day moving average lines and MACD plot. MA is the abbreviation for Moving Average.

The requirement for the bullish pattern of the stock is that the low in the stock price is above the previous lows. This is illustrated in Fig. 6.1 by drawing a straight line joining the inflexion points A and D and intersecting the stock price curve at F. If anyone of the inflexion points on the stock curve on the right side of D would be below this straight line, then the straight line would be redrawn so at to join the point A with this lower inflexion point. In the present case, the intersection of the straight line with the stock price curve at point F would indicate that the prior bullish pattern of the stock is being broken. This is what happened indeed because the stock sold off after point F making lower and lower inflexion point in every cyclic step.

It should further be noted that the 50-day and 200-day moving average lines are brought closer together only when the stock price dips suddenly. In many cases, the 50-day moving average line may dip below the 200-day moving average line. *All of these patterns are indicative of the bearish behavior of the stock.*

The MACD plot for XYZ stock is shown in the lower part of Fig. 6.1. It was obtained by clicking on MACD in the 'Add Indicator' location. Notice that it shows a cyclic behavior around a datum line marked 0 on the vertical scale on the right. MACD crosses the base line zero at the point corresponding to point A' on the stock price curve and stays positive while going up and down until it crosses the base line again corresponding to point E on the stock price curve. Notice that the stock price was in the up mode from point A' to point E. Afterwards the stock price dipped and then MACD became negative. MACD became positive after May 14 when the stock resumed increasing again. It should thus be noted that the plot of MACD makes understanding the stock behavior much easier. It is also useful for investing decisions keeping the following in mind:

So long as MACD stays above the datum (zero) line, stay invested in the stock. Follow the stock behavior closely if MACD is ready to go negative and get out of the stock if needed. Similarly, again follow the stock closely when MACD, while on the negative side, starts decreasing and is close to crossing the datum line so as to become positive. This may be an appropriate time to get back into the stock.

It should be noted that the moving averages show what stock prices have already done, not what they will do. The same applies to MACD because it is a function of the moving averages. Predicting future price behavior from the past behavior is not an exact science and requires a lot of personal judgment. It has also the likelihood of being wrong. *For this reason, it is strongly recommended that the technical analysis be used in coordination with the fundamental analysis so as to reduce the likelihood of error.*

6.7 Technical Analysis Applied to a Hypothetical Stock ABC

Figure 6.2 shows the technical chart for another hypothetical stock, say ABC. It shows the zigzag curve for the stock price, two moving average (MA) lines, and the volume of stock traded which is represented by the vertical bars on the horizontal axis. For the moving averages, the periods of 10 and 50 days, which are shorter than the commonly used 50 and 200 days, were selected because shorter periods reflect the change in stock price earlier.

The difference in the moving average periods does not change the interpretation of the stock price trend. The figure covers the time period of one year. The diagram shows the increase in stock price from A to B during which period the 10-day MA line is above the 50-day MA line. The divergence between the two moving average curves corresponds to the section A-B of the MACD plot shown also in Fig. 6.2. Note that MACD oscillates around the zero line between the bounds of +1.0 and -1.0 shown on the vertical axis. Since the gap between the two MA lines has been increasing from A to B, the MACD curve bound by the vertical lines shows diverging pattern and is on the positive side of the zero axis. This indicates the bullish trend for the stock price. Beyond point B, the 10-day MA drops down steeply and so the lines corresponding to 10 day and 50 day moving averages tend to converge. This is shown by B-C on the MACD plot and this is indicative of the bearish behavior. At point C the MACD curve crosses the zero line and goes into the negative territory. This represents the beginning of the long period during which the 10-day MA has stayed below the 50-day MA. This represents the bearish stock behavior. In October 2010 the two MA lines almost merged which is also reflected in the MACD plot corresponding to this period. At pint D the 10-day MA curve starts climbing more steeply than the 50-day MA curve. This corresponds to the point where MACD changes from negative to positive. This represents the bullish behavior. Thus the segments A-B and D-E on the MACD curve are associated with the increase in stock price. As such the investor would be well advised to get out of the stock at point B on the MACD curve, get in at point D and get out again at point E. *The usefulness of the technical analysis in providing the signals for entry and exit in and out of a specific stock is thus obvious.*

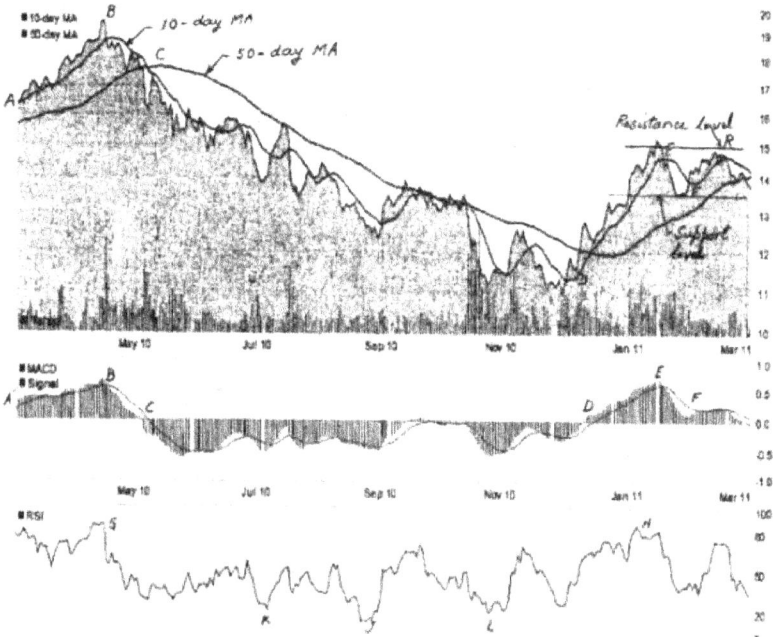

Fig. 6.2 Technical chart showing the stock price variation and trading volume for hypothetica ABC stock over a period of one year along with 10-day and 50-day moving average lines, MACD and RSI plots.

The bottom part in Fig. 6.2 shows the RSI plot. Here the points G and H indicate the overbought condition and the points J, K and L the oversold condition. Since the RSI plot provides overbought and oversold conditions frequently during the year, the usefulness of the curve is limited basically to short-term traders.

6.8 Support and Resistance Levels

The market technicians often talk about the price support and resistance levels for a stock. The support level refers to the price level from which the stock bounced up during the preceding drop in price. Referring to the stock price curve in Fig. 6.2, it can be seen that the stock price fell from E to F and then bounced back up. Thus the point F established the support level for the stock. From this level, the price of stock rose to point R and then dipped again. The level corresponding to point R is called the resistance level. If the stock price breaks through the resistance level during the next up cycle, that will establish a new resistance level. Likewise new support and resistance levels will be generated due to the cyclic variations in stock price. When the stock oscillates repeatedly in a narrow price range, the phenomenon is known as the *accumulation*. From this level, the stock may break to go up or down. If it goes up, it is considered fairly bullish and that merits consideration for buying the stock.

6.9 Summary

1. Technical analysis makes use of the concept that stocks with strong momentum in one direction stay in that direction for extended periods of time.
2. The stock price movement in the up or down direction is the result of supply and demand imbalance which is affected by the perception of the investors based on the news and their personal evaluation.
3. Technical analysis uses a number of parameters. Those covered in this chapter are the moving averages, MACD and RSI.
4. Moving averages tend to smooth out the fluctuation in stock price on a daily basis and indicate the overall direction of the stock price movement.
5. MACD is a technical parameter which fluctuates around a base line. Its direction from negative to positive indicates the likelihood of the stock going up and vice versa.
6. RSI is a technical parameter that indicates the overbought and oversold conditions of the stock.

7. The requirement for the bullish pattern of the stock is that the low in the stock price should stay above the previous lows.

Suggested Action Items

Factor in the technical analyses for the four companies analyzed in the earlier chapter and see if your decision to invest in the companies selected could have been different.

Chapter 7

Sectors and Industries for Investment

7.1 Introduction

In this chapter, we will be looking at the sectors and the businesses in them with the perspective of their suitability for investment. We will be examining the scope and operation of these entities so as to understand how they make money and where they fit in the economy. We will look at the effect of demographics and economy on the potential of these entities for turning out profits. A brief description of the various sectors is also included along with the names of some companies in each sector.

7.2 Classifying Industries

Investors sometimes speak about the industries and the sectors interchangeably. However, there is a distinction between the two. In general, a sector is a broader term which can include several different industries. In the same way, an industry can include several different subindustries. For the sake of illustration, let us consider the auto industry with which most people are familiar. The auto industry belongs to the industrial sector, and it is comprised of many subindustries. The latter are in the business of supplying the automobile companies with different components such as the engine, transmission, door and body, seat, airbag, electronics, battery, etc.

Standard & Poor's (S&P) and MSCI developed an industry classification system. It is called the Global Industry Classification Standard (GICS). It divides the companies into the following major sectors:

1. Consumer Discretionary
2. Consumer Staples
3. Energy

4. Financials
5. Health Care
6. Industrials
7. Information Technology
8. Materials
9. Telecommunication Services
10. Utilities
11. Real Estate Sector

Within this framework, there are 24 industry groups, 67 industries, and 156 subindustries.

An alternative classification, known as the Value Line Investment Survey Industry Classification, was introduced earlier in Chapter 5 and given in Table 5.1.

In following sections, we will be looking at the S&P sectors and the major industries in them. In order to invest in them, we need to have broad understanding of the nature and scope of these businesses along with the factors that affect them.

7.3 Consumer Discretionary Sector

This sector deals with the products and services that the public would like to have but does not necessarily need to survive. In this sector are the companies producing consumer items that people buy because they want to and not because they need to. Some of the examples of the consumer discretionary companies are fast-food restaurants such as McDonald's Corp (MCD) and Panera Bread (PNRA), entertainment products and services companies such as Walt Disney (DIS) and Electronic Arts (EA), and automobile companies such as Ford Motor (F) and General Motors (GM). Included are also the retail stores such as Macys (M), Target (T) and Walmart (WMT) which sell both consumer discretionary and consumer staples items.

The sales and profits of the consumer discretionary companies are dependent upon the economy. These companies thrive only when the economy is good. The discretionary products and services do not sell well if the consumers are worried about the economy. Such companies have limited pricing power

because of the competition and pressure from supermarket chains which sell their products at thin margins. These companies have limited growth prospects, at best close to the GDP growth. The stocks of these companies are reliable but slow growers and so are suitable for the investors who want a long term steady return.

7.4 Consumer Staples Sector

This sector deals with the consumer items which are the necessities as opposed to being discretionary, as in the earlier section. The examples of such items are food, beverages (both alcoholic and non-alcoholic), prescription drugs, personal care items, household items, tobacco products, etc. These are the items that people would like to have regardless of their financial situation. As such the stocks related to these are considered non- cyclical, meaning that they are in demand, no matter how the economy is performing. Hence these companies keep producing at a regular pace and are thus able to generate steady sales and profits. The examples of some large consumer staple companies are The Kroger Co. (KR), Colgate-Palmolive (CL), General Mills (GIS), Kraft Heinz (KHC), Proctor & Gamble (PG), Kimberly-Clark (KMB), Coca-Cola (KO), CVS Health (CVS), Caremark, Under Armour (UA), Nike (NKE), Sketchers USA (SKX), Home Depot (HD), Lowes (LOW) and Altria Group (MO). Also included in this sector are the supermarket chains such as Target (TGT) and Walmart (WMT) which sell both the consumer discretionary and the consumer staples.

The companies in the consumer staples sector have wider moats than those in the consumer discretionary sector and have better pricing power as well. While considering to invest in these companies, the items to look for are the popularity of their products that would ensure good revenues and profits, needs for capital expenditure, free cash flow and the return of cash to shareholders in the form of dividends and stock buybacks.

7.5 Energy Sector

the business of producing energy from all the types of resources such as coal, oil, gas, wind and solar. Though coal is the most common, it is not the because of the competition and pressure from supermarket chains which sell their products at thin margins. These companies have limited growth prospects, at best close to the GDP growth. The stocks of these companies are reliable but slow growers and so are suitable for the investors who want a long term steady return.

7.4 Consumer Staples Sector

This sector deals with the consumer items which are the necessities as opposed to being discretionary, as in the earlier section. The examples of such items are food, beverages (both alcoholic and non-alcoholic), prescription drugs, personal care items, household items, tobacco products, etc. These are the items that people would like to have regardless of their financial situation. As such the stocks related to these are considered non- cyclical, meaning that they are in demand, no matter how the economy is performing. Hence these companies keep producing at a regular pace and are thus able to generate steady sales and profits. The examples of some large consumer staple companies are The Kroger Co. (KR), Colgate-Palmolive (CL), General Mills (GIS), Kraft Heinz (KHC), Proctor & Gamble (PG), Kimberly-Clark (KMB), Coca-Cola (KO), CVS Health (CVS), Caremark, Under Armour (UA), Nike (NKE), Sketchers USA (SKX), Home Depot (HD), Lowes (LOW) and Altria Group (MO). Also included in this sector are the supermarket chains such as Target (TGT) and Walmart (WMT) which sell both the consumer discretionary and the consumer staples.

The companies in the consumer staples sector have wider moats than those in the consumer discretionary sector and have better pricing power as well. While considering to invest in these companies, the items to look for are the popularity of their products that would ensure good revenues and profits, needs for capital expenditure, free cash flow and the return of cash to shareholders in the form of dividends and stock buybacks.

7.5 Energy Sector

the business of producing energy from all the types of resources such as coal, oil, gas, wind and solar. Though coal is the most common, it is not the preferred source because of the emissions generated which are harmful to the atmosphere. Oil is the most preferred resource because of its versatility for use in cars, motorcycles, tractors, airplanes, portable devices such as lawn movers and snow blowers, etc. Natural gas is preferred over oil because it burns cleaner but is limited in terms of the use for space heating and to a limited extent for transportation. The alternative sources of energy such as wind and solar are much cleaner and so are gaining momentum as the preferred sources of energy but their contribution is miniscule compared to the oil and gas because of the cost disadvantage.

Related to the oil, there are different kinds of companies. There are the companies dealing with the exploration and production which extract oil from deep strata on and off land and lately from shale deposits. Then there are companies which refine, transport and market the refined products. When crude oil is refined, it produces gasoline, jet fuel and lubricants which are all marketable products. The companies that are involved in all of these businesses are known as the *integrated* companies and the examples of such companies are ExxonMobil (XOM) and Chevron (CVX). The examples of the companies in the exploration and pumping of oil from the underground are Conoco Philips (COP), ExxonMobil (XOM), BP (BP), Total S.A. (TOT) and Chevron (CVX). The examples of the companies in the refining business are Valero (VLO) and ExxonMobil (XOM). Refining is a lower profit business than the extraction of oil from ground. The crude oil extracted from the ground or shale deposits is transported to the refineries by ships, trucks, rail and pipelines. The pipeline companies are paid like a utility and so generate a steady stream of cash flow. This enables the pipeline companies to pay generous dividends to stockholders. Some pipelines are owned by the major oil companies while some of them, such as Kinder Morgan (KMI), are independent.

In addition to the above companies, there are companies which perform seismic studies in locating the underground deposits and perform the services related to drilling and maintaining wells. The examples of the major companies in these services are Schlumberger (SLB), Halliburton (HAL) and Baker Hughes (BHI). Additionally, there are companies engaged in the construction of energy-related equipment.

The current emphasis is on the generation of energy from clean alternative sources such as wind and sun. The most efficient process for generating electricity from the sun is using photovoltaic cells. There are now solar farms which have a vast area covered with photovoltaic cells so as to generate large amounts of energy. The wind power energy is generated using the turbines and similar to the solar farms there are wind farms. The problems with both solar and wind energy are the cost and the contribution to the total energy needs.   The examples of some of the companies in solar energy are First Solar (FSLR), SunPower Corporation (SPWR), SolarCity (SCTI), Trina Solar (TSL) and Yingli Green Energy (YGE). The examples of the companies in the wind market are GE Energy (GE), Vestas Wind Systems (VWDRY) and Gamesa (GAM.MC). The companies in the solar and wind power are volatile in terms of the investment.

The energy sector is highly cyclical in nature and is sensitive to the changes in consumer demand as well as the geopolitical events. The stocks in the energy sector are highly correlated to the price of the commodities such as crude oil and natural gas. They suffer also from the risk that some cheaper technology may be developed.

7.6 Financial Sector

This is a broad sector consisting of the banks, asset management and insurance companies which are described below.

7.6.1 Banks

The banking system is vital for any country. The banks support the economy by lending money to the customers and businesses. They profit from lending money to borrowers for big ticket items such as financing home, car, furniture, appliances, etc.   Since they lend at rates higher than their costs, the difference contributes to their profits.   In addition to this, they make money by charging customers the fees for items such as low balance, insufficient funds, transfer of funds, rents on safe deposit boxes, and underwriting fees for mortgages, etc. The banks have the facility to borrow from the Federal Reserve Bank at rates much cheaper than the market. The Federal Reserve Bank also helps the banks by providing   FDIC   insurance on customer deposits. In return the banks are required to satisfy the minimum capital requirements imposed by the Federal Reserve. The latter also puts restrictions on the amount of dividends they can pay to stockholders.

There are two kinds of banks: national banks and regional banks. The regional banks do business in a specific region of the country which may involve many states. The national banks are much bigger and operate nationally and abroad. The names of some of the national banks are Citigroup (C), J.P. Morgan (JPM), Bank of America (BA) and Wells Fargo (WFC). Some of the major regional banks are Athens Bancshares (AFCB), Investors Bancorp (ISBC), Simmons First National (SFNC), Trico Bancshares (TCBK), Heritage Financial (HFWA), Home Bancshares (HOMB) and Union Bankshares (UBSH).

When considering investment in a bank, the investor needs to examine a number of items: balance sheet, loan categories, underwriting standards, non-performing loans and charge-off rates. The non-performing loans are those on which the borrowers are not making payments. The charge-off rates measure the percentage of loans that the bank does not expect to be paid back. The information about charge-off rates and non-performing loans is available in the Annual and Quarterly Reports of the banks to the Securities and Exchange Commission.

7.6.2 Asset Management

The asset management business involves managing the clients ' money by investing in diverse financial instruments such as stocks, bonds, mutual funds and private equity. The clients are individuals, pension funds, institutions and similar other entities. The investment managers charge fees for this service. This is big business dealing with billions of dollars. Such services are offered by the asset management firms as standalone businesses or within a bank or a trust company. The fees for such services vary and are normally about 1% of the investment amount. Even such small fee rates generate a huge profit because of the large assets being managed. The business of asset management has a wide moat because it requires expertise in money management. Some of the big asset management firms are BlackRock (BLK), UBS Group (UBS), Credit Suisse (CS), Goldman Sachs (GS) and Morgan Stanley (MS). The big banks such as J.P. Morgan (JPM), Wells Fargo (WFC) and Citigroup (C) also have asset management groups. While considering to invest in an asset management company, the items to look for are the past track record, diversity of investments, and the size of the assets being managed.

7.6.3 Insurance

In any kind of insurance, the objective is to protect the asset from the unforeseen losses in lieu of the premium paid by the insured. For example, the life insurance companies offer protection to the dependent survivors from premature death of the bread winner. Similarly the disability insurance provides benefits if the insured becomes disabled. In the case of Property and Casualty insurance, the protection is offered for the damages caused by natural disasters such as fire, lightning, tornado, hurricane, floods, earthquake, etc. In every case, the insurer pools money from the premiums of policy holders, invests in safe products and covers the unforeseen risks from the money so accumulated. The examples of the insurance companies are State Farm, MetLife (MET), Prudential (PRU) and Aflac (AFL). The examples of the property and casualty insurance companies are Progressive (PGR) and Berkshire Hathaway (BRK-B) subsidiary GEICO.

Insurance is a complex and risky business because of the uncertainty associated with pricing of the unknown events. Thus while investing in an insurance company, this uncertainty should be taken into consideration. The insurance companies suffer from considerable regulation and intense competition, and have low returns. In the selection for investment, the track record of the company becomes a very important factor. In addition to this, the items to look for are the financial strength, size of the assets, risk level, revenue and profit growth, return on equity and the market leadership.

7.7 Healthcare Sector

People need health care irrespective of the economy. As such the companies in this sector are not affected by the economy. This makes it a defensive area for investment in bad economic times. The companies in this sector benefit from the Government programs such as Medicare and Medicaid and the subsidy to the insurance premiums. The businesses in this sector may be put in the following three categories:

7.7.1 Pharmaceutical Companies

Because of the patent protection on new drugs for a number of years, the pharmaceutical companies are immune from competition during this period. On the expiry of the patent protection, the generic formulations of these patented drugs come into the market and this hurts the profits of the patented drug company. Thus, while considering to invest in a drug company, the investor needs to pay special attention to the loss in revenue from patent expirations. The drug companies such as Merck (MRK), Pfizer (PFE), Baxter International (BAX) and Abbot Labs (ABT) were very profitable at one time but have suffered lately because of the expiry of drug patents and the lack of promising drugs in the pipeline. Their profitable position has now been taken over by the biotechnology companies such as Celgene (CELG), Gilead Sciences (GILD), Biogen (BIIB), Amgen (AMGN) and others. These are hot investments at present, some with lofty valuations but are highly volatile.

The pharmaceutical industry has a great economic moat because of the high start-up costs and patent protection. This is so because bringing a drug into the market takes many years involving the research, multiphase testing and approval from the FDA. Thus the companies that are suitable for investment are only those that have blockbuster drugs with patent protection, a pipeline of promising drugs for serious diseases with high sales potential, strong record for the development of new drugs along with strong sales and marketing capabilities. They need to be financially strong to support the development of new drugs as well.

The generic drug companies are not good investment because of the lack of patent protection on generic drugs and the possibility that the same generic drug may be brought into the market by other companies. The generic drugs are priced much cheaper and so their profit margins are fairly small.

7.7.2 Medical Device Companies

These companies are in the business of developing implants such as the pacemakers and the knee and hip joints. Similar to the patented drugs, these implants too need extensive development, testing and evaluation for the FDA approval and they too have patent protections. This gives medical device companies a wide moat and great pricing power. The FDA approval process for these implants is not that rigorous as for the drug companies. A minor improvement in materials and/or design qualifies them for a new patent. The medical device companies are currently benefitting from a great demand by the aging population. Some of the companies in this category are Medtronic (MDT), Johnson & Johnson (JNJ), Baxter International (BAX), Abbott Laboratories (ABT), Boston Scientific (BSX), General Electric (GE) and Stryker Corp (SYK).

7.7.3 Health Insurance and Managed Care Companies

These companies issue health insurance policies and thus act between the healthcare providers and the families needing health insurance. Since the healthcare providers want to maximize their profits and the policy holders want maximum coverage for the lowest premiums, the companies work with fairly narrow margins. As such they lack pricing power and try to capitalize on the numbers insured. They have intense competition and are subject to government regulatory control. They suffer as well from cost controls by the Government funded programs such as Medicare and Medicaid. Some of the companies in the managed care business are Aetna (AET), Cigna (CI), HCA Holdings (HCA), and Humana (HUM).

7.8 Industrial Sector

The industrial sector is the biggest contributor to the economic well being of a nation. It includes a broad array of companies that make equipment and machinery and also perform related services. The following is a partial listing of the industries in this sector:

Aerospace - Airlines and Defense

Marine equipment and services

Capital goods

Construction and engineering

Building materials

Industrial machinery

Construction and Farm machinery

Trucking

Roads, Railroads, Rail tracks

Transportation – rail and trucking

Electrical equipment

Office services & supplies

In the industrial sector, there is intense competition and so the pricing power is limited. Thus the industries in this sector capitalize on volume. The fortunes of the businesses in this sector depend upon the economy. When the economy is good, the demand for travel is higher. This leads to the increased air and rail travel and the purchases of automobiles, leisure goods and services. With the increase in air travel, the airline profits are higher. This enables the airline companies to buy more planes which results in greater demand for materials such as specialty metals for engines, aluminum alloys and polymer composites for plane bodies. The planes need tires, seats, brakes and electronic, hydraulic and navigation systems and so the demands for related materials and services is increased. The aerospace industries such as General Dynamics (GD), United Technologies (UTX), Raytheon (RTN), Northrop Grumman (NOC) and Lockheed Martin (LMT) also prosper in good economic times.

The greater demand for goods and services results in increased trucking, rail transportation, production of consumer items and the related equipment needed to produce them. There is housing boom which adds to the demand for building materials, electrical items, heating and air conditioning equipment, appliances, etc. The development of infrastructure is higher and this increases the demand for construction materials and heavy equipment such as cranes, earth moving equipment, tractors and loaders etc. This adds to the profits of companies such as Caterpillar (CAT), Terex (TEX), Manitowoc (MTW) and Deere (DE) which make earthmoving equipment, cranes, tractors and agricultural machinery.

7.9 Information Technology and Artificial Intelligence Sector

This sector is related to the companies that involve the application of computers to store, retrieve, transmit, and manipulate vast amounts of data for specific tasks thereby achieving the economies of scale. The companies in this sector develop software for the manipulation of data for fields such as the internet, applications, systems, database management, and the technology consulting and services. The industries associated with the information technology sector are computer hardware, software, data storage, semiconductors, internet software and services, telecom equipment, e- commerce and computer services. Related to the artificial intelligence are the industries related to the design and production of the chips such as Nvidia, Qualcomm, Advanced Micro devices, Intel, Taiwan Semiconductor Manufacturing, ASML, SK Hynix and Samsung Electronics etc.

Information technology is a hot field. There are a host of industries and businesses related to this field. Some of the companies in this sector are Accenture (CAN), Amdocs (DOX), Amkor Technology (AMKR), Apple (AAPL), Amazon.com (AMZN), Cisco (CSCO), Hewlett Packard (HP), International Business Machines (IBM), Microsoft (MSFT), Oracle (ORCL), Facebook (FB), Fiserv (FISV), Google (GOOGL), Intel (INTC), Skyworks (SWKS), Symantec (SYMC), Infosys (INFY) etc.

While considering the investment in the information technology sector, one should keep in mind that these companies are subject to fast product cycles, price competition and technological advances. This requires a solid management with a record of innovation and development and with the ability to lead into the introduction of new technology and products along with strict cost controls to stay competitive. The investor should look specifically at the company product, its appeal to the masses, economic moat and the competitive advantage, and the financial ability of the company to support new technology and development work.

7.10 Materials Sector

This sector is related to the industrial materials, both metallic and non-metallic, and their alloys and composites. The basic metallic materials are aluminum, copper, brass, steel, magnesium, nickel, zinc etc. and their alloys such as stainless steel and tool steel. Then there are non-metallic materials such as polymers which are made from petroleum. Polymer composites are the polymers reinforced with materials such as carbon and glass. The basic materials and their alloys are used for making machine components and the structural components as in the automobile and airplane bodies. The consumption and the demand for these materials is therefore dependent on the demand for industrial machinery and structures. Since this demand is related to the economic cycle, the stocks of materials are also dependent upon the economy. When the economy is good, the companies in the industrial

sector are producing goods at a rapid rate and so the demand for materials is high. It is this demand that contributes to the fortunes of the companies in the materials sector.

The examples of some of the companies in the materials sector are:

Southern Copper (SCCO), Rio Tinto (RIO), Barrick Gold (ABX), Goldcorp (GG) - mining companies dealing with various metals

Alcoa (AA) – aluminum

Arcelor Mittal (MT), Nucor (NUE), US Steel - steel

Freeport-McMoRan (FCX) - various metals Dow

Chemical (DOW) - chemicals

Potash Corp (POT) mining company producing potash for fertilizer Air

Products and Chemicals (APD) – industrial gases

The industrial materials have low economic moat because of the slim profit margin, cyclic demand and competition from the industries here and abroad. Thus the path to prosperity is low cost production and high asset utilization. The materials sector is the old economy sector with hard assets and high fixed costs. It does not make a good investment unless the company is in the development of new and advanced materials such as advanced composites, carbon nanotubes, etc. Some materials companies such as Monsanto (MO) and 3M (MMM) have created moats over the years. Monsanto used to produce commodity plastic materials but later got into the development of genetic seeds. 3M Co, which is known for scotch tape, has developed numerous patents of specialized products and this has given it the moat. Thus while looking for investment in this sector, one should look for the companies with a niche of their own.

7.11 Telecommunication Services Sector

Long time ago, this sector was a monopoly of the Ma Bell companies. At that time these companies provided only the basic landline telephone service and operated just like any other utility. That has changed completely over the years and we have now the wireless and broadband internet phone service. The telecom industry has experienced huge growth as more and more people are using its services. There is always the risk of introduction of new communication systems and devices with time. The companies in this sector create a steady stream of revenue by locking subscribers into contracts of years. However, the competition is so severe that it has because very easy to switch from one provider to another with the help of incentive from the new service provider.

The companies in this sector are not very attractive for investment because of the large capital needs for upgrading, regulation, intense competition and so very limited pricing power. The pace of technological change has allowed several new types of competitors to threaten the once-secure position of telecom companies. The development of wireless companies and broadband Internet phone services have cut into the reliable cash flows and earnings of
the traditional telecommunications providers. The technological risks with telecom stocks grow as innovative new communications systems and devices appear.

The telecommunication companies are suited for the investors looking for dividends because they operate just like a utility collecting reliable monthly payments for the services provided. Their yields are generous and reliable. Some of the companies in this sector are CenturyLink,T&T (T), Verizon VZ), Mediacom Communications (VZ) etc.

7.12 Utilities Sector

The companies in the utilities sector are in the business of supplying electricity, gas and water to the households and businesses. The sector is dominated by the electric utilities which are involved in the generation of electricity from coal, natural gas, nuclear material, hydroelectric, wind and solar energy. These companies also facilitate the transmission and distribution of the electric energy to their customers. The electric utilities are heavily regulated. For example, the power plants using coal and natural gas as the fuel are regulated by the Environmental Protection Agency (EPA). The nuclear plants are regulated by the Nuclear Regulatory Commission (NRC). The utility rates are regulated by the state agencies. Lately the trend has been towards increasing deregulation. The deregulated utilities have the flexibility to charge more when the supply of energy is tight.

The electric utility stocks with the exception of nuclear energy are considered safe investments. The nuclear utilities are riskier because the radiation hazard can devastate them. The utilities with solar and wind as the sources of energy are also risky because they depend upon the government incentives to compete. The utility stocks pay regular dividends (often generous) but have very little growth potential. They are thus an investment option for retirees who need safety and a regular stream of income coming from dividends. Some of the names of the public utility companies are American Electric Power (AEP), NextEra Energy (NEE), Pinnacle West Capital Cp. (PNW), PG&E Corp. (PCG), Northwestern Cp. (NWE) and Teco Energy (TE).

While considering investment in a utility, the investor should pay special attention to the balance sheet and the debt outstanding. A strong balance sheet is needed to ensure that the company will be able to upgrade to meet the regulatory requirements as well as pay regular dividends. The utilities with the record of increasing dividend with time are more desirable. The cutbacks in dividends are a warning signal because that may signal trouble and so the time to get out of the stock.

7.13 Real Estate Investment Trusts

The businesses described here belong to the real estate sector which was added to the GICS classification in August 2016. These are organized as trusts which benefit from the special tax code. As such these are known as the real estate investment trusts (REITs). These trusts own and in some cases operate the commercial properties such as shopping malls, hotels, office buildings, commercial properties, hospitals, warehouses, timberland, etc.

They are required by law to distribute at least 90% of their earnings to the investors which makes them attractive to dividend-seeking investors. They can deduct these dividends from their earnings which enables them to avoid most of their tax liabilities. Instead the investors pay taxes on the dividends they receive. Some of the dividend is treated as the return of capital in which case the investors do not have to pay taxes on this part of the dividend. The untaxed dividends reduce the cost basis to the investors and so the taxes are paid by the investor on the capital gains when the shares are sold. REITs trade like stocks on the stock exchanges.

There are many kinds of REITs:

1. Equity REITs – These own the real estate properties such as the shopping malls, office buildings and apartment complexes which are leased to the tenants. The income comes from the rents which is distributed as dividends to the investors. In addition there is capital appreciation or loss when these properties are sold. The other kinds of REITs are timber REITs and pipeline REITs where the earnings come from the sale and rental of the facilities. The majority of REITs are equity REITs. Examples: Avalon Bay Properties, Inc. (AVB), Boston Properties (BXP), American General Hospitality Corp (AGT), Cabot Industrial (CTR), General Growth Properties (GGP), etc.

2. Mortgage REITs – These invest in the property mortgages. They either loan money for mortgages to real estate owners or purchase mortgages or mortgage-backed securities. Their earnings come from the difference between the interest they earn on the mortgage loans and the cost of funding these loans. These are

highly sensitive to interest rate increases. Some of the examples are American Capital Agency Corp. (AGNC), Annaly Capital Management Inc. (NLY) and Apollo Residential Mortgage, Inc. (AMTG).

3. Hybrid REITs – These are the hybrids of the upper two because they invest in both the properties and the mortgages. The examples of such REITs are AG Mortgage Investment Trust (NYSE:MITT), Invesco Mortgage Capital (NYSE:IVR), American Capital Mortgage Investment Corp (NASDAQ:MTGE) and Chimera Investment Corp (NYSE:CIM).

7.14 Master Limited Partnerships

These are similar to the REITs in that they do not pay taxes and are able to pass the tax obligations to the investors. They are thus able to pay a large portion of their earnings as dividends and hence their appeal to investors. A master limited partnership (MLP) is a publicly traded business which derives most of its income from real estate, natural resources or commodities. It has two types of partners: limited partners and a general partner. The limited partners provide capital to the MLP and receive periodic income distributions from the MLP's cash flow. The general partner is responsible to manage the partnership. The Master Limited Partnerships are primarily in the energy arena such as pipelines, crude oil storage, refined product storage, exploration and production of oil or gas, coal production and the like. Some of the biggest MLPs are Enterprise Products Partners (EPD), Williams Partners (WPZ), Magellan Midstream Partners (MMP) and Energy Transfer Partners (ETP). When picking the MLP for investment, look for the one with growing business and a strong history of distribution increases.

7.15 Summary

1. The Global Industry Classification Standard (GICS) divides the companies into ten major sectors which are the Consumer Discretionary, Consumer Staples, Energy, Financials, Health Care, Industrials, Information Technology, Materials,

Telecommunication Services and Utilities.

2. A sector includes several industries and an industry may have different subindustries.

3. The consumer discretionary sector includes items which people buy at their discretion basically for their pleasure as they are not necessarily needed.

4. The consumer staples sector is related to the items which are the necessities in everyday life. As such the industries in this sector thrive even in bad economic times.

5. Energy sector is a broad sector consisting of the industries in oil exploration, refining and distribution and power generation from nuclear, solar and wind. It is a cyclical sector because the fortunes of the companies are tied to the supply and demand of the energy.

6. The financial sector consists of the banks, asset management and insurance companies. The banking sector is very important for the economy of the country and the stocks in this sector are steady growers. Asset management is a big business dealing with billions of dollars and is fairly lucrative for the financial sector.

7. Healthcare sector consists of the pharmaceutical and medical device companies, hospitals and health/managed care insurers. This is a thriving sector irrespective of the economy.

8. The industrial sector is vast in terms of its scope and consists of the industries dealing with land and air transportation, farming and construction equipment and machinery, maritime and defense needs, equipment and supplies for power generation, etc.

9. Information technology is a part of our everyday life involving computers, communication, internet, recreation, etc. With newer breakthroughs every day, it is hard to imagine what life will be a few years down the road. The companies in this sector are hot in terms of the investment but volatile due to obsolescence from newer developments.

10. The materials sector deals with the exploration and refining of all kinds of materials – metals, polymers and ceramics. Since the material needs depend upon the economy, the stocks in this sector are economically sensitive.

11. The telecommunication services and the companies supplying electricity, gas and water have similar characteristics. They are

practically the utilities needed in everyday life. Since these companies collect monthly charges for the utilities provided, they are relatively stable in terms of the dividend payment. They do not have a large potential for growth.

12. The latest addition to the GICS sector classification system is the Real Estate Sector. It includes the real estate trusts and other real estate companies.

Chapter 8

Investment in Bonds and other Fixed Income Securities

8.1 Introduction

This chapter deals with the fixed income securities, mainly the bonds. It describes the underwriting process and the bond-issuing entities. It discusses the bond ratings and the terminology relevant to the trading of bonds. It describes the various kinds of bonds including the Federal Government Securities and Government Agency Securities. It explains the factors that affect the fluctuation in bond prices. It provides also the guidance on the selection of fixed income securities.

8.2 Fixed Income Securities

In general, the debt securities with a fixed interest rate are known as the fixed income securities. The most common investment in this category is a Certificate of Deposit (CD). It is available from the banks, the credit unions and the brokerages in varying amounts and with different maturities. It is backed by the Federal Deposit Insurance Corporation (FDIC) for up to $250,000 per person and $500,000 in a joint account. The interest rate on a Certificate of Deposit is fixed for its term. Similar to the certificates of deposit, some financial institutions offer the notes and the commercial paper which are available for investment. The US Treasury sells the treasury bills which have the maturities of less than one year.

Bonds are the most common debt securities used by the investors to diversify their portfolios and meet other investment objectives. These are the debt securities (or IOUs) which means that the investors buying bonds are not buying the share in an entity but are instead loaning money to it.

Bonds are also used by the corporations and the government bodies to raise capital for specific purposes. Bond holders receive a return on their investment in the form of regular interest payments, typically paid every six months, followed by a final payment at maturity. This final payment is equal to the *face value* of the bond and the interest for the last six month period. The mandatory interest payment feature entitles bonds to be called the "fixed income" instruments. The risk involved with bonds is that the borrower may run into financial difficulty during the term of the bond thereby risking the payment of principal and this makes the credit-worthiness of the borrower very important. The bonds are rated for credit-worthiness by the credit agencies and the rating plays an important role in determining the bond yield. As creditors the bondholders have the first claim, ahead of the owners of common or preferred stock, in the event of bankruptcy. Bonds are highly liquid investments because they can be readily sold in the market as and when required. In this case, the sale price, which could be more or less than the principal amount, would depend upon the prevailing interest rates and the date of maturity.

8.3 Procedure for the Issuance of Bonds

The borrower (known as the *issuer* of bonds) does not sell bonds directly to the public. Instead, the bonds are marketed through investment bankers such as Goldman Sachs, Merrill Lynch, Morgan Stanley, etc. The investment banker, called the *underwriter*, acts as an intermediary between the issuer and the investing public. The formal terms of the bond sale are drawn up by the lawyers in a legal document, known as the indenture. The terms are in compliance with the regulations of the Securities and Exchange Commission (SEC). The major terms of the indenture are described in the prospectus.

To illustrate the process, let us say that the State of New York needs to borrow $100 million in order to finance a road project. The State publicizes its intention to issue the bonds and invites bids. The investment bankers submit their bids to the State either individually or jointly in a group, known as the *syndicate*. The State reviews the bids and makes its determination for the award. The underwriter then handles all aspects of the sale. The investors are usually the large institutions such as the banks, insurance companies and pension funds as well as some individual investors.

The role of the underwriter ends after the bonds have been sold. The bookkeeping functions such as the payment of interest and the redemption of principal are handled by a fiduciary agent which could be a bank or some other financial institution.

8.4 Agencies Issuing Bonds

The bonds are issued by the different agencies described below:

1. Federal Government - The securities issued by the federal government include the treasury bills, notes and bonds, treasury inflation-indexed securities (TIPS), zero coupon bonds, and savings bonds. Treasury securities make up the largest sector of the bond market.

2. Government Agencies - There are more than fifteen government-sponsored agencies (GSEs) that issue bonds. Some of the largest agencies are the Federal National Mortgage Association (commonly known as Fannie Mae, FNMA), the Federal Home Loan Mortgage Corporation (referred to as Freddie Mac), and the Student Loan Marketing Association (known as Sallie Mae). Some of the other GSEs are the Federal Home Loan Bank, the Federal Farm Credit Bank, the Agency for International Development, the US Maritime Administration and the Export- Import Bank.

The agencies such as the Fannie Mae and the Freddie Mac buy residential mortgages from the banks and other lending institutions and pool them into mortgage-backed securities (MBS) for resale to the investment community. Similar to the mortgage-backed securities are the asset-backed securities (ABS) which deal with other types of debt such as the credit cards and auto loans. An ABS can be created from almost anything that has material and predictable future cash flows.

3. Public Entities - The municipal bonds are sold by the States and their political subdivisions which include the counties, cities, and public authorities. The examples of the public authorities issuing such bonds are the utilities, educational institutions, housing authorities and transportation systems.

4. Corporations – The corporate bonds are issued by the companies to

   finance expansion or raise capital for other needs. The bonds that are secured by the specific assets of a company are recognized as the senior debt. The bonds that are not secured by the physical assets but are issued on good faith of the company are known as the debentures.
5. Foreign Governments and Corporations – The foreign issuers can also register bonds in the USA. These bonds are called the Yankee bonds. The Yankee market typically consists of the bonds issued by the Canadian Provinces, Canadian companies, European governments and large multinational companies.

8.5 Bond Ratings for Safety

Since the bonds are long-term investments, they suffer from the default risk, the only exception being the securities backed by the US Treasury. The credit-worthiness of the issuer is thus an important consideration in the selection of the bond for purchase. In order to assist the buyers in this regard, the bonds are rated for credit quality by three agencies which are the Standard & Poor's Corporation (S&P), the Moody's Investor Service Inc. and the Fitch Inc. Table 8.1 gives

Table 8.1 Bond rating categories

Moody's	S&P	Fitch	Grade
Aaa	AAA	AAA	Investment
Aa	AA	AA	Investment
A	A	A	Investment
Baa	BBB	BBB	Investment
Ba	BB	BB	Speculative Grade
B	B	B	Speculative Grade
Caa	CCC	CCC	Speculative Grade
Ca	CC	CC	Speculative Grade
C	C	C	Speculative Grade
D	D	DDD, DD, D	Default

The bond ratings provided by these agencies. Here triple-A rating is of the highest quality and the rating in each successive line goes down one step below. Thus, in the investment category, triple-A is the highest and triple-B (or Baa) the lowest ranking for credit quality. Similarly, the gradation of credit quality goes down for each successive step in the speculative grade. The D category indicates that the debt is in default. Sometimes, + or – may be appended to the letter grade to show the relative ranking within a category.

The bonds rated BB (S&P and Fitch), Ba (Moody's) and lower are known as the junk bonds. These bonds carry high risk and high yield. This area of the market is known as the high yield market. On the other hand, bonds rated double A to triple A are referred to as the high grade bonds.

Some bonds carry insurance to cover the payment of interest and principal in the case of default. There are many agencies which insure bonds. The agencies with the highest ratings are Assured Guaranty, FSA, and Berkshire Hathaway. Ambac and MBIA have carried AAA ratings from Moody's and Standard & Poor's. The weaker insuring agencies are CIFG, FGIC, and XLCA. Note that the value of insurance depends up the insurer's ability to make good on its obligation to make the timely payments of interest and principal if needed.

8.6 The Terminology of Bonds

The following terminology applies to bonds. The terms are presented below in an alphabetical order:

1. Accrued Interest - It is the interest that has been earned by the bond-holder but not yet paid by the bond-issuer since the last coupon payment.
2. Coupon Rate – It is the stated rate of interest on the bond. It is fixed for the life of the bond. The interest payments are made every six months.
3. Cusip Number- It is a nine-digit number assigned to the bond for precise identification.
4. Call Feature – It refers to the provision in the indenture that allows for early forced redemption of the bond, often at a premium to its face value. This feature enables the issuer to retire expensive debt by taking advantage of the prevailing lower interest rate. The bonds with call feature have a series of call dates (typically once per year) at which they can be called. US Treasuries do not have the call feature.
5. Call Premium – It is the extra amount paid by the bond issuer if the bond is called before the maturity date. This is an incentive to make callable bonds attractive to the investors who would otherwise prefer to own non-callable bonds.
6. Duration – It is the term used to gauge the sensitivity of bond to interest rate changes. It is used to predict how much a specific bond will go up or down in price if interest rates change. It is explained in Section 8.9.
7. Face Value (also called the principal or par value) - It is the amount borrowed by the issuer.
8. Maturity Date (also known as the redemption date) – It is the date on which the last interest payment is made and the face value of the bond repaid.

9. Redemption Value – It is typically the same as the face value of a bond. However, for a callable bond, it is the face value plus the call premium.

10. Settlement Date – It is the date on which the ownership of the security changes hands. Typically, this is several days after the trade date. In the US, the settlement date is usually 3 days after the trade date.

11. Sinking Fund – It refers to the provision in the bond for repayment where the bond issuer retires a portion of the bond at regular intervals over the life of the bond.

12. Yield – There are three kinds of yields: current yield, yield to maturity, and yield to call. They are described below:

   (a) Current Yield – It is the annual interest payment divided by the current market price of the bond.

   (b) Yield to Maturity (YTM) - It is the compound average annual expected rate of return if the bond is purchased at its current market price and held to maturity. It assumes that the interest payments are reinvested for the life of the bond at the same yield. YTM is an important parameter because it enables the comparison between two bonds.

   (c) Yield to Call (YTC) – It is the yield calculated assuming that the bond will mature at the next call date. It is also known as the Yield to First Call. When the yield to all call dates is calculated, the yield in the worst-case is known as the Yield to Worst.

The change in yield is often given in terms of the *basis points*. A basis point equals one-hundredth of a percentage point. For example, a decline in yield from 5.15% to 5.10% is equal to a decline of 5 basis points.

8.7 Types of Bonds

The following terminology is used to describe the various kinds of bonds:

1. Asset-Backed Bond – It is the bond securitized by a financial asset.

2. Bearer Bond – It is the bond that does not have the owner's name registered on the books of the issuer and is payable to the bearer of the bond.

3. Collateral Trust Bond – It is the bond protected by lien against the issuer's property which is usually a portfolio of the securities held in trust by a commercial bank.
4. Collateralized Mortgage Obligation Bond – It is a mortgage-backed security in which the cash flow from a mortgage pool is distributed at varying rates of return, based on the bondholder's class or level of investment.
5. Convertible Bond – It is the bond with provision that allows conversion between the issuer's bond and the common stock at some fixed exchange rate.
6. Floating Rate Bond – It is the bond in which the interest payments are allowed to change over the life of the bond based on some financial benchmark.
7. High Yield Bond – It is the bond rated below the investment grade which is Baa by Moody's or BBB by Standard & Poor's. Such bonds are also known as the Junk bonds.
8. Municipal Bond – It is the bond issued by a municipality when funds are needed either to run the local government or to build and maintain specific projects such as highways, bridges or sewage treatment plants.
9. Serial Bond – It is the bond issue with multiple maturities which are staggered over a number of years.
10. Stripped Bond – Such bonds have coupons stripped from the bonds and both parts are sold separately.
11. Zero Coupon Bond – This is the bond which makes no interest payments during the term of the bond. In lieu of this, it appreciates in value as the maturity date approaches. This type of bond is sold at discount to the face value and is redeemed at the face value on maturity

8.8 Trading of Bonds at Premium or Discount

When a bond is issued, it has a unique Cusip number, face value, coupon rate and the date of maturity. The coupon rate determines the amount that will be received every six months in terms of the interest payment. This amount is fixed for the life of the bond. The current yield, called the market yield, differs from the coupon rate and fluctuates with time because it depends upon the current interest rate, economic conditions, and the supply and demand situation. The difference between the coupon rate and the market yield accounts for the difference in the current price of the bond and the face value of the bond. When the coupon rate and the market yield are identical, the bond price will be equal to the par value. Let us say that the coupon rate is 6%, so the bond with a par value of $1000 will be paying $60 per year. If the market yield declines to 5.5%, the bond price rises to compensate for the higher payment of $60 received (because interest payments depend upon the coupon rate which is 6%) compared to $55 that is available based on the current market yield. In other words, the bond is now trading at a premium. Similarly, if the market yield rises to 7%, the bond price will fall in order to adjust to the market conditions because an investor can currently get $70 in the market whereas this bond is still paying only $60 per year. The bond in this case will now be trading at a discount. From the above discussion, it is seen that price of a bond is interest-rate sensitive, typically rising when the interest rates are falling and vice versa.

Fixed income securities trade, for the most part, on the basis of their yield. The price of the security is interest-rate sensitive, typically rising when interest rates are falling and vice versa. They are also affected by the coupon rate, the term to maturity and the credit quality. The level of the coupon rate determines, in part, how much a bond goes up or down in price when interest rates change. The change is greater in the case of a bond with lower coupon rate than that for a higher coupon rate. With longer term to maturity and lower credit quality, the uncertainty of payment increases and that also affects adversely the bond prices. These are the important factors deserving of attention in dealing with `bonds.

8.9 Bond Duration

Duration is a way of measuring how much bond prices are likely to change if and when interest rates move. In other words, it provides a measure of the interest rate risk. It should be realized that if the general interest rate increases, the bond price adjusts downwards to make the bond coupon payment compatible with the prevailing interest rate.

For the same reason, if the interest rate decreases, the bond price adjusts upward. In other words, the bond will have a lower sale price in the first case and higher in the latter case.

The concept of duration is useful because it enables the bond purchaser to evaluate how much interest rate risk is associated with the particular bond or bond fund purchase. The duration is based on the same cash flows as yield to maturity (YTM) but also takes into account the interest on interest. The bond with a coupon rate makes payments every six months based on the yield to maturity. So if the yield to maturity is 4%, a bond with a principal value of $10,000 will make $200 payment every six months (that is a total of $400 every year). These payments may be invested on receipt at the prevailing interest rate. Thus the bond holder is earning not only the coupon payment but also the interest payments on these coupon payments as and when they occur. Because of this, the average time to receipt of the cash flows is less than the time to maturity.

Understanding duration is particularly important for those planning to sell bonds prior to maturity. If you hold the bonds to maturity, you get the coupon payments as well as the principal payment of $10,000 on maturity regardless of what happens with interest rates. If, however, you sell that bond before maturity (or if you are invested in a fund that buys and sells bonds while you own it) then the price of your bonds will be affected by the changes in interest rates.

The general guideline is that for 1% change in interest rate, the price of bond will go up or down by the duration number. The longer the duration of a bond, the greater is its volatility. Bonds with lower coupons have longer durations than those with larger coupons. For zero coupon bonds, the duration and maturity are the same as there are no coupon payments during the term of the bond.

8.10 Call and Put Options

Some bonds include embedded options in their indenture. The most widely used is the *call option*. The call option gives issuer the right to call the entire issue, or parts thereof, at his/her discretion.

This option is exercised to the advantage of the issuer when the issuer can borrow at cheaper rate than the coupon rate of the bond. On the other hand, this option is detrimental to the bondholder because the principal redeemed can be invested only at the current cheaper market rate. The other option is the put option. The bond with this option is called the putable bond. This bond gives investor the option to redeem the bond at the predetermined price .The put price and the redemption date are spelled out in the indenture.

8.11 Federal Government Securities

These securities are issued by the US Treasury and are the direct obligation of the US Government. So there is no redemption risk. The treasury securities, commonly known as the "Treasuries", are sold through auction by the Federal Reserve Bank. These are highly liquid securities and can be readily sold in the secondary market. These securities are exempt from the state taxes.

There are many kinds of federal government securities which are described below:

(a) Treasury Bills, Treasury Notes and Treasury Bonds

Treasury bills (popularly known as the "*T-bills*") are short-term instruments. They are auctioned with the original maturities of 4-weeks, 3-months, 6- months and 1-year. The US Treasury auctions 3- and 6-month T-bills on Mondays, 4-week T-bills on Tuesdays, and 1-year T-bills on a monthly basis. The T-bill is a non-interest bearing instrument: it is sold at a discount from par and redeemed at par. The difference between the par (face value) and the discounted price paid is its yield. For further details, refer to the TreasuryDirect website given below:

http://www.treasurydirect.gov

Treasury Notes come in three maturities: 2 years, 5 years, and 10 years. They pay interest every six months. The auctions for 2-year notes are held at the end of each month, and those for 5- and 10-year notes every quarter.

Treasury Bonds have maturities often to thirty years. They pay interest every six months. They are sold through a bidding system which uses competitive and non-competitive bids. With a non-competitive bid, the buyer agrees to accept the yield determined at auction. Here the buyer is guaranteed to get the bond he/she wants and in the full amount desired. With a competitive bid, the buyer specifies the yield that he/she is willing to accept. Depending upon the yield determined at auction, the buyer may or may not get the bond or the amount of the bond may be less than the amount desired.

The noncompetitive bids are placed either directly at TreasuryDirect or through a bank, broker or dealer. The competitive bids are placed only with a bank, broker or dealer. The procedure to submit direct bid to the treasury is described at the TreasuryDirect web site given above.

(b) Treasury STRIPS

These are zero coupon bonds constructed by taking a treasury note or treasury bond and stripping off the interest coupons. They are sold at deep discount to their face value. The interest payments are made here only at maturity. They are quoted and traded on a yield-to-maturity (YTM) basis and the yield on STRIPS is generally higher than on other instruments of the comparable maturities. They are subject to phantom income tax which means that even though the interest is not paid at regular intervals, the investors have to pay the income tax on accrued interest. They can be bought and sold only through a financial institution, broker or dealer.

(c) Treasury Inflation-Indexed Securities (TIPS)

The principal on TIPS is adjusted with the changes in the Consumer Price Index. With inflation (a rise in the index), the principal increases; with deflation (a drop in the index), the principal decreases. Whereas TIPS pay interest at a fixed rate, the interest payments vary in amount from one period to the next because the principal on which interest is paid changes. Thus, with inflation the interest payment increases, with deflation the interest payment decreases. The interest payments are received by the investor every six months at the adjusted rate. At maturity the investor receives the adjusted principal or the original principal, whichever is greater. This provision is meant to protect the investor from the effects of inflation and deflation.

The procedure for buying the TIPS is similar to that for the treasury bonds and is described at the TreasuryDirect website given above.

(a) US Savings Bonds

The US government markets the savings bonds for small investors. These bonds can be redeemed by the treasury any time after an initial holding period of six months. EE savings bonds are one of the most popular treasury issues. They have a minimum investment of $25 as opposed to $1,000 for other treasury securities. They sell at 50% discount to their face value and the interest is paid only at maturity. The interest rate compounds on a semiannual basis and is adjusted half yearly to 90% of the average yield on 5-year treasury securities for the preceding six months.

The HH savings bonds are different from the EE savings bonds in that the HH bonds provide current income and are issued at full face value. The interest rate is fixed and the interest payments are made every six months. They can be obtained only in exchange for the E or EE savings bonds.

Series I savings bonds are bought at face value and are inflation-indexed. The interest rate on these bonds is composed of two separate rates: a fixed rate of return and a variable semiannual inflation rate. The interest is accrued and added to the principal monthly and paid only at redemption.

Both the EE and I series bonds can be purchased to qualify for the education tax exclusion. This means that these bonds can be used to save for a child's education tax-free.

For detailed information on these bonds as well as the procedure to buy these bonds, refer to the following website

http://www.savingsbonds.gov

8.12 Government Agency Securities

These securities are issued with the objective of reducing borrowing costs for the homeowners, farmers, students and others. The federal agencies that sell debt instruments are classified as the government-sponsored enterprises (GSEs). They were created by the Congress to provide benefit to the specific segments of the society and are not government entities. They issue debt in order to raise capital which is loaned to the borrowers at cheaper rates and at more favorable conditions than those available in the market. The credit rating of this debt is very high but not guaranteed by the US Treasury. The yields of the bonds issued by these agencies are higher than those of the treasury bonds and so these securities are fairly attractive to the investors.

The securities offered by the government-sponsored enterprises are described below:

(a) Fannie Mae (FNMA), Freddie Mac and Ginnie Mae (GNMA)

Fannie Mae and Freddie Mac are GSEs and are regulated by the Housing and Urban Development Department. Their charter is to help the low and moderate income families in buying homes. These agencies issue discount notes to raise capital which is used to buy mortgages from the lenders. The agencies package some of these loans into mortgage-backed securities (MBS) which are then resold to investors. By doing so, these agencies provide liquidity to the housing market. During the financial crisis of the years 2007 – 2009, the mortgage guarantors Fannie Mae and Freddie Mac needed massive bailouts and were placed in conservatorship of the US Government in September 2008.

Ginnie Mae (GNMA) is different from Fannie Mae and Freddie Mac. It is a U.S. government corporation within the U.S. Department of Housing and Urban Development (HUD). Its charter is to ensure liquidity for the government-insured mortgages, including those insured by the Federal Housing Administration (FHA), the Veterans Administration (VA) and the Rural Housing Administration (RHA). The Ginnie Mae mortgage-backed securities (MBSs) are guaranteed by the FHA, which are typically the mortgages for first-time home buyers and low-income borrowers. Ginnie Mae does not issue, sell or buy pass-through mortgage-backed securities. It simply guarantees the timely payment of the principal and interest from the approved issuers (such as the mortgage bankers, savings and loans, and commercial banks) of the qualifying loans.

Similar to the mortgage-backed securities, there are collateralized mortgage obligations (CMOs) which are issued by the brokerage firms. These bonds are backed by a trust created to hold the Ginnie Mae and other government-guaranteed mortgages. The advantage of these bonds lies in their minimum investment requirement of $1000 compared to $25,000 for the Ginnie Maes and they also have slightly higher yields.

(b) Federal Home Loan (FHL) Bank System

The three basic parts of this system are a group of 12 banks, the Federal Housing Finance Board which regulates them, and the Office of Finance, which acts as a liaison with Wall Street. Over 8,000 community financial institutions are members/shareholders in the FHL Bank system. The mission of the FHL Banks is the following:

(i) To provide cost effective funding to the members for housing, community, and economic development

(ii) To provide regional affordable housing programs which create housing opportunities for the low and the moderate-income families

(iii) To support housing finance through the advances and the mortgage programs

(iv) To serve as a reliable source of liquidity for its membership.

The banks issue short-term, non-callable, discount securities in minimum amounts of $50,000 and long-term bonds. Any bond issued to raise capital is a joint obligation of all twelve FHL banks and so has a high degree of security.

(c) Farm Credit System

It is a nationwide financial cooperative that lends money and provides the financial services to agriculture and rural America. Congress created the System in 1916 to provide American agriculture with a dependable source of credit. Farm Credit makes loans and leases at competitive rates with flexible terms to fit the needs of farmers, ranchers, commercial fishermen, agribusinesses and country home owners. The banks in the system issue three kinds of securities: short-term discount notes in a minimum denomination of $50,000 for 5 to 270 days; short-term bonds with maturities of 3-9 months in a minimum denomination of $50,000; and medium-terms notes with maturities from one to ten years and a minimum denomination of $1000.

(d) Student Loan Marketing Corporation (Sallie Mae) – This GSE provides federally guaranteed student loans originated under the Federal Family Education Loan Program.

In addition to the above, there are other agencies such as the Resolution Funding Corporation (REFCORP) and the Tennessee Valley Authority (TVA) which were created by the Congress for specific purposes.

8.13 Municipal Bonds

These bonds are issued by the states, local governments, and special public entities such as the school districts, transportation systems, utilities, and sewer and housing authorities, Most municipal bonds (often called the 'munis') are exempt from the federal income taxes while some are subject to the alternative minimum tax. The latter are known as the AMT bonds. Some muni bonds are exempt from the state tax in the state in which issued. The bonds issued by the US territories, namely, Guam, the Virgin Islands, and Puerto Rico are exempt from the federal taxes as well as the state taxes in all the states. The exemption from taxes makes municipal bonds attractive for high-income tax payers.

The equivalent yield-to-maturity of the municipal bonds is calculated using the following equations for comparison to the yield provided by the corporate bonds that do not have the tax exemption advantage:

(a) For municipal bonds with no state tax exemption

Taxable equivalent bond yield = (tax-exempt municipal bond yield)/ (1 – marginal federal tax rate)

Here the marginal tax rate is the highest federal tax bracket applicable to the tax payer.

Thus for an investor in the 28% marginal federal tax bracket, the taxable equivalent yield on a 5% municipal bond will be equal to 5/(1- 0.28) = 6.94%.

(b) For municipal bonds with state tax exemption

If the bond is exempt from both the federal and state taxes, then we first calculate the effective state tax rate using the following equations:

Effective state tax rate = Marginal state tax rate x (1 – marginal federal tax rate)

Combined marginal tax rate = Effective state tax rate + marginal federal tax rate

Taxable equivalent bond yield = Tax-exempt municipal bond yield/ (1- combined marginal tax rate)

Example: Consider a marginal state tax rate of 9% and marginal federal tax rate of 28%.

Here the effective state tax rate = 9 x (1- 0.28) = 6.48%. Thus the combined marginal tax rate is 28 + 6.48 = 34.48%, and the taxable equivalent yield on the municipal bond is = 5/

(1- 0.3448)

= 7.52%.

The above calculation shows that because of the federal and state tax-exempt status of the bond, the equivalent bond yield is 7.52%. In other words, this municipal bond is equivalent to a corporate bond with 7.52% yield.

It should be noted that for the same municipal bond the taxable equivalent yield will be even higher for an investor in the 35% marginal federal tax bracket (7.69% without state tax exemption, and 12.24% with state tax exemption). Thus the municipal bonds make very attractive investment for the investors in high income tax brackets.

There are two types of municipal bonds:

(a) General Obligation Municipal Bonds - These bonds are supported by the taxing power of the issuing entity such as the state, county or city.

(b) Revenue Municipal Bonds - These bonds are supported by the specific revenue streams. The examples of revenue bonds are transportation bonds, water and sewer bonds, housing bonds, convention and casino bonds, hospital bonds and highway bonds. In addition to these, there are tobacco bonds which represent a kind of securitized debt instrument supported by the proceeds from tobacco companies under a legal settlement.

The bonds may be either coupon bonds or zero coupon bonds. Coupon bonds pay interest at the coupon rate in two six monthly installments. Zero coupon bonds do not have a coupon rate because these do not pay regular interest but instead the interest in included in the pricing of bonds. Thus a zero coupon bond with a face value of $10,000 is priced much lower than its face value but on redemption it pays $10,000.

Some municipal bonds are offered with attractive security enhancements known as the escrow or pre-refunded features. In this case, the issuer places a predetermined amount in a bank or escrow account to meet the obligations of the outstanding bond. On the same lines some bonds are insured against defaults. The leading insurance companies are Municipal Bond Insurance Association (MBIA), Financial Guaranty Insurance Company (FGIC), AMBAC Indemnity Corporation (AMBAC) and Financial Security Assurance Holdings Ltd. (FSA).

8.14 Corporate Bonds

The corporate bonds are issued by the corporations such as banks, finance companies, brokerage houses, insurance companies, real estate investment trusts, utility companies, railroads, airlines, and manufacturing and service related companies. These corporations may be put in four groups: finance companies such as banking and insurance; utilities; industrials; and transportation companies. Similar to the corporate bonds are the Yankee bonds which are foreign bonds that are dollar denominated so that the currency risk is eliminated. These bonds are issued and traded in the USA like other bonds. Similar to the Yankee bonds, there are Brady bonds which are issued by the emerging market countries. Most corporate bonds are fixed rate but some are issued with floating rates as well. In the case of floating rate bonds, the coupon rate is reset periodically, usually every six months, based on a benchmark interest rate.

The corporate bond market is huge. These bonds are bought by the institutions and individuals both. They come in a wide range of maturities. The rating symbols for the corporate bonds are similar to those for the municipal bonds. The Standard and Poor's rates corporate bonds for events under a special rating system called the "event risk covenant rating". Here the bonds are rated from E1 to E5 where E1 represents the lowest degree of protection and E5 the highest. The short-term corporate debt, which is called the commercial paper, has its own set of ratings, as given by the Standards and Poor's. These ratings are A (highest quality) to D (lowest quality) where "A" is further divided into A1 to A3 in decreasing order of strength.

Bonds with the ratings of BB (S&P) or Ba (Moody's) or lower are called the junk bonds and this market is called the high-yield debt market. The main feature of these bonds is that they provide higher yields than those from other debt instruments but are fairly risky in terms of the default rate. For this reason, the investment in junk bonds at individual level is not recommended. Instead one should consider investing in these bonds with mutual funds because they provide professional management as well as diversification.

Credit protection is important for corporate bonds because the companies can fail for a variety of reasons. This protection is offered in the form of securities. For example, a utility company may issue a bond secured by the first mortgage on one of its properties and this will appear in the bond title as XYZ Power Company, First Mortgage Bonds. Similarly there are collateral trust bonds which may be secured by the securities of the subsidiaries of the bond-issuing company. The guarantee may also be in the form of equipment trust certificates, bank letters of credits, or insurance. The unsecured bonds are called the debentures or notes. They are protected by the credit of the company issuing the bond. Corporate bonds are also subject to leveraged buyouts or takeovers which present liquidity problems and increased uncertainty.

Similar to the municipal bonds, the corporate bonds may be callable or non-callable. The callable bonds are likely to be called when the issuer can finance its operations at cheaper rates. Some bonds have extraordinary call features where the call feature is triggered by specific events. The bonds may have sinking fund feature, which means that a certain percentage of bonds have to be retired every year regardless of the interest rate consideration. Some corporate bonds have putable feature which allows the bondholder to resell the bond at par to the issuer before maturity. Unlike the municipal bonds, a corporate bond may have the convertible feature which means that the bond can be turned in for shares of the company as per details in the indenture.

Corporate bonds have higher yields than those of the municipal bonds but are taxable at all levels - city, state and federal. Considering the taxation aspect, the advantage of corporate bonds over municipal bonds may be lost depending upon the income tax bracket of the bond buyer. In general, the corporate bonds are suitable for the non-taxable accounts of high-income tax payers, but low-income tax payers may find them advantageous in taxable accounts as well.

Similar to the corporate bonds, some corporations sell direct access notes (DANs) which have fixed interest rates and come in various maturities ranging from a few months to many years.

8.15 Fluctuation in Bond Prices

Bond prices are affected by the state of the economy. The latter affects the economic well-being of the corporations, the states and the nation. When the economy is poor, the credit risk is increased and so the bonds prices change to compensate for this risk. In order to spur the economy, the Federal Reserve Bank often cuts the discount rate. This results in lowering the market interest rate which increases the bond prices. When the inflation increases thereby hurting the economy, the Federal Reserve Bank increases the interest rate by decreasing the money supply. With the increase in interest rate, the bond prices decrease. It should be noted that the market interest rates are affected by many factors. Since there is a balancing action to keep the economy on track, the market interest rates may fluctuate back and forth. In addition to the interest rates, the bond prices depend upon the supply and demand as well. For detailed discussion see Chapter 14 on the Economic Factors in Investment Decisions.

The consideration of the above factors is important for bond investors. For example, if the bond yields are trending higher, it would be prudent to wait for the uptrend to take effect before committing new funds. If the bond yields are at their peak, the investment in non-callable, zero-coupon, long-term debt securities of maximum safety (such as the treasury bonds) should be considered. The increase in inflation will require the tightening of money supply resulting in higher interest rates so the bond prices will fall. The magnitude of the drop in prices depends upon the bond duration. The higher the duration, the larger is the drop in price. As such in the scenario of increasing interest rates, the investment in the bonds with shorter duration is more desirable.

The prediction of the economy and the direction of the movement in bond prices on a consistent basis is not possible. This is so because the economic indicators are often revised and it is only after the indicators are out that one can confirm the state of the economy. For example, recession is confirmed only after two successive quarters of negative GDP growth and so the confirmation of recession is well after the event. The economists often use the yield curve for prediction of the economy. The yield curve is the plot with the yield plotted on the vertical axis and the maturity of treasury securities plotted on the horizontal axis. There are three basic shapes of the yield curve:

1) Upward sloping where the long-term rates are higher than the short-term rates

2) Downward sloping where the short-term rates are higher than the long-term rates

3) Flat where the short-term and the long-term rates are equal.

The upward sloping curve is most common. It indicates that higher rates are expected in the future due to the expected economic upturn, as at the tail end of recession, that is several quarters later. The downward sloping curve indicates worse economic conditions in future such as the expected recession four to six quarters later. The flat curve indicates that the fast-growing economy is being restrained as in the case of impending inflation. The flat curve is transitory and will finally change either to an upward or downward slope.

8.16 Which Bond to Buy

The answer to this question depends upon the needs of the investor. Bonds are used for diversifying the investment portfolio so as to have a balanced portfolio of stocks and bonds in addition to the cash instruments. In a portfolio of the bonds only, the diversification in bonds is also important.

Since the interest rates and the economic conditions affect the return from bonds, consider building a ladder of bond investments with different maturities in your fixed-income part of the portfolio. Here some bonds mature every few years and this makes it possible to invest the proceeds into other bonds of about the same or different maturities. This strategy enables the investor to invest the proceeds from the matured bonds at the prevailing interest rate thereby reducing the effect of changing economic conditions on the return from bonds.

For the investor in a high-tax bracket, the investment in municipal bonds with high credit rating (A or higher) should be considered. The tax-exemption feature of the municipal bonds is likely to provide a higher equivalent yield than that obtained from the other bonds. If living in a state with income tax, the possibility of buying a municipal bond with state tax-exemption should be looked at. Note that all the bonds issued in the state are not allowed the benefit of state tax exemption. On the other hand, the municipal bonds issued by the US Territories such as Puerto Rico and Guam are granted exemption from the state taxes.

The following comments are provided as the general guidelines for fixed-income investing:

1. In any investment decision, risk and reward go hand in hand. Often the higher the risk, the higher is the return and vice versa.

2. For short term needs, consider investing in CDs, treasury bills and money market funds. They provide maximum safety. For comparison of the national CD and money market fund rates, search the internet site http://www.BankRate.com.

3. For two to five years and maximum safety, consider treasury notes. Alternatively consider investing in Ginnie Maes which are guaranteed by the Treasury but share price fluctuation occurs on a daily basis. So a no-load Ginnie Mae mutual fund with low cost might be the right choice.

4. For longer durations, consider treasury notes, treasury bonds, STRIPS, or corporate bonds with high safety rating.

5. If inflation is expected to rise, check out the return on TIPS. One can invest here in a no-load mutual fund with low cost.

6. Junk bonds provide higher returns at the expense of safety. They are too risky to invest unless diversified. For this reason, one should consider investing a small part of the portfolio in junk bonds through a mutual fund for the sake of diversification.

7. The investment in foreign bonds directly is not advised because of the extra risks involved arising from the currency fluctuation, instability of governments, social problems, and shaky economic conditions.

8.17 Procedure for Buying Fixed Income Securities

(a) CDs and Money Market Funds

The certificate of deposits are sold by the banks, credit unions and brokerage houses. The money market accounts are opened with banks and credit unions. For the best rates, investors can consult the website http://www.BankRate.com/.

(b) Treasury securities

These securities may be purchased directly from http://www.treasurydirect.gov through the bidding system as discussed in Section 8.10. These can also be purchased from the banks and the brokerage houses for a nominal commission. The procedure for buying the US Savings Bonds is given on http://www.savingsbonds.gov. STRIPS are bought and sold through a financial institution, broker or dealer.

(c) Municipal bonds and Corporate bonds

These bonds are bought through a brokerage house. So the first step is to open a brokerage account if that is not already the case. On the brokerage website in the fixed income section, there is a listing of the bonds available for trading. One can search the bonds that meet the investor's criteria. Here you specify your preferences some of which are the term of maturity, credit rating, coupon or yield, and call protection.

In the case of municipal bonds, you may specify the state and the purpose (such as housing, education, public service, health care, etc). You may specify the constraints such as general obligation, revenue, taxable, subject to AMT, insured, putable, etc. These choices are shown collectively in Exhibit 1 for Municipal bonds. The corresponding exhibit for Corporate bonds is shown in Exhibit 2.

Exhibit 1. Express Search for Municipal Bonds

Issue

CUSIP List

Ranges

	Minimum	Maximum
Maturity		
Moodys/S&P Ratings:	Baa/BBB ▼	▼
Quantity		
Coupon		
Yield:		
Price:		
Call Protection		
Delivery	All ▼	

☐ Exclude

Interest Payment Frequency:

Use Ctrl-Click to select multiple frequencies.

All
Semi-Annually
Annually
Quarterly

☐ Exclude

States

Use Ctrl-Click to select multiple states.

All States
Alabama
Alaska
Arizona
Arkansas

☐ Exclude

Purpose

Use Ctrl-Click to select multiple purposes.

All Bonds
Housing
Education
Public Service
Health Care

☐ Exclude

Coupon Payments

Use Ctrl-Click to select multiple months.

December
All Months
January
February
March

☐ Exclude at maturity

Constraints

	Yes	No
General Obligation	☐	☐
Revenue	☐	☐
Callable	☐	☐
Tobacco Settlement	☐	☐
Pre-Refunded	☐	☐
Escrowed to Maturity	☐	☐
Taxable	☐	☐
Subject to AMT	☐	☐
Insured	☐	☐
Bank Qualified	☐	☐
Putable	☐	☐

Display Properties

Sort by:	Maturity ▼
Rows per page:	50 ▼
Updated Since: (Eastern)	

The following items deserve attention:

1. Maturity decision is made considering the duration for which you want your funds to be invested in this bond.
2. For the credit rating, it is suggested to stick to 'A' or better because bonds with poor ratings carry a lot of risk considering the long term investment in the bonds. With junk bonds, there is too much risk of the default and so the investment in them is advised only through mutual funds which provide instant diversification.

3. You may specify either the coupon rate or the yield. The coupon rate is important if you want the interest payments in a specific amount at regular intervals. Whereas the amount of interest payment is fixed, the yield changes with the price of the bond.

4. For the state tax exemption benefit in a municipal bond, you will have to specify your state of residence. Sometimes you may get a better return on a bond from a different state and so you must check this out providing your preference as "All States".

5. You may provide the purpose of the bond if you so desire.

6. In terms of the constraints, pay special attention to the entries such as 'callable', 'taxable' and 'subject to AMT'. Further note that 'insured' provides the extra layer of safety. The tobacco settlement bonds should be avoided because of the risk that the tobacco companies may not be able to provide funds at a future date in view of the litigation risk and the ever decreasing population of the smokers leading to reduced profits. Be careful that specifying too many parameters limits the choices and this may hurt the return. Instead specify the minimum necessary parameters so that you are presented with a wide range of choices. You may then narrow down your selection based on your preferences.

8.18 Interpreting the Bond Quotes

· The typical quote of a municipal bond is given below:

Municipal Bond: Cusip: XXXXXXXXX
Laguna Salada CalifUN School District G.O. Bond Type:

General Obligation, Non-Callable

Ratings: Baa3/A, Insurance: FGIC Tax
Status: Tax Exempt
Offer Qty: 45, Minimum Qty: 10 Price:

$54.409, Coupon: 0.000

Yield to maturity: 5.08%; Maturity: 08-01-2020

This is a municipal bond for the school district in California. It is a non-callable general obligation zero coupon bond which means that the regular interest payments will not be made on this bond. The bond matures on August 1, 2020. It has the yield to maturity of 5.08%. It has a rating of Baa3/A and is insured by the FGIC Co.

The bond is being sold at discount and the price on maturity will equal the par value of the bond. *Note that the bonds are sold in $1000 multiples so that the par value or principal value of one bond is $1000.* Since the minimum quantity for purchase is 10 bonds, the price collected on maturity of these 10 bonds will be 10 x $1,000 = $10,000.

As for the purchase price, it should be noted that the market prices of bonds are quoted as a percentage of the bonds' par value. So on $10,000 par value the price will be (54.409/100) x 10,000 = $5,440.90 (ignoring commission).

· The example quotation for an old corporate bond is given below:

Cusip: YYYYYYYYY, National City BK Louisville KY MTN
Non-Callable, Coupon: 6.300, Pay Frequency: Semi-Annual, Maturity: 02-15-2021
Ratings: A3/A

Dated Date: 02-15-1996; First Coupon: 08-15-1996 Offer Qty: 94, Min Qty: 10: Settlement Date: 06-18-2008 Price: 96.648; Yield to Mat: 7.713; Current Yield: 6.519
Principal: $9,664.80; Accrued Interest: $215.25; Total Dollars: $9,880.05

This is the quotation for the corporate bond of National City Bank Louisville Kentucky. It is non-callable. It is a coupon bond with the interest coupon rate of 6.3% which will be paid semiannually. The minimum quantity for purchase is 10 bonds which at the offer price of $96.648 would cost

(96.648/100) x10,000 = $9,664.80. For the settlement date of 06-18-2008, the accrued interest is $215.25. So 10 bonds would cost $9,880.05 which is the sum of the principal $9,664.80 and the accrued interest of $215.25. Note that 10 bonds have a face value of $10,000 but are being offered for $9,880.05. This means that the bonds are being sold at discount. Since it is a discount bond, the yield to maturity is 7.713% which is higher than the coupon rate of 6.3%.

8.19 Summary

1. The fixed income securities are the certificate of deposit, notes, commercial paper and treasury bills. They do not have any default risk.

2. Bonds are the debt securities issued by the corporations and government agencies intended to raise capital for specific projects. They carry a fixed interest rate and have a fixed maturity date but can be sold anytime in the market.

3. Just like stock prices, bonds fluctuate in prices which means that there are possibilities to either make or lose money in the bond market.

4. The securities issued by the Federal Government are treasury bills, treasury inflation-indexed securities (TIPS), zero coupon bonds and savings bonds etc. In addition to this, there are a large number of government agencies which issue the bonds. Some of these agencies are Fannie Mae, Freddie Mac, Sallie Mae, Federal Home Loan Bank, Federal Farm Credit Bank etc. They are all meant to help a particular segment of the society. For example, Fannie Mae and Freddie Mac help the low and moderate income families in home financing. Sallie Mae provides federally guaranteed student loans.

5. The public entities such as the States, counties, cities, utilities , educational institutions, housing authorities and transportation systems issue municipal bonds which are exempt from the federal taxes and in some cases the state taxes too.

6. The corporate bonds are issued by the companies or businesses to finance their operation.

7. The bonds are rated by the agencies such as Moody's, Fitch and S&P. The investment grade bonds carry ratings from AAA to BBB and the speculative grade bonds carry BB to C ratings. The bonds in default carry ratings D to DDD.
8. The bond prices are affected by many factors some of which are the economy, interest rate, supply and demand, credit risk, etc.

Suggested Action Items

On your broker website, analyze how two corporate bonds, one investment grade and another junk category, with different durations fared in increasing interest rate environment.

Chapter 9

Investment in Mutual Funds

9.1 Introduction

Mutual funds have been the favorite investment product of both the small and large investors. They make it possible for the people with no investing experience to invest their money in stocks and/or bonds. Since these funds consist of a large number of stocks and/or bonds in their portfolio, they provide the benefit of diversification as well. As the funds pool money from a large number of investors, they provide an economical way to manage the investors' money for a nominal cost. Since the retirement benefits of most people are invested in mutual funds, the understanding of the structure and the types of funds would help people in making prudent decisions in selecting the proper funds for their retirement accounts. With the advent of ETFs which are covered in the next chapter, the popularity of mutual funds is on the decline.

9.2 The Concept of Mutual Funds

Mutual funds pool money from a large number of investors and invest it in the stocks, bonds and other assets. The pooled money is invested by the money managers in the specific kinds of investments which are described in the prospectus of the fund. If the money is invested in stocks, the fund is known as the stock fund. If it is invested in bonds, the fund is known as the bond fund. If the money is invested in stocks and bonds both, it is a hybrid mutual fund. The large combinations that are possible with the types of investments, the variety of stocks in terms of the capitalization, industry, value and growth, domestic and international, and the types of bonds such as the municipal bonds, taxable bonds, domestic and international bonds etc. gives rise to the large categories of mutual funds. When invested in mutual funds, the investors own shares in the fund in proportion to their investment in the fund.

There are a large number of mutual fund families which offer mutual funds invarious categories.The name of the fund includes the name of the fund family and a specific name which is indicative of the types of investments in the fund. For example, the Vanguard Capital Appreciation Fund tells us that the mutual fund company managing this fund is Vanguard and the objective of the fund is capital appreciation. Another example of a mutual fund is the Fidelity Magellan Fund which tells us that the fund belongs to the Fidelity family but the name Magellan does not tell us about the type of investments. In this case, one needs to read the prospectus of the mutual fund to find the investment style of the fund. There are a large number of mutual fund companies, some of them with very large numbers of mutual funds. Some of the examples in this category are Fidelity, Harbor, Pimeo, T. Rowe Price, Vanguard, ete. The listing of mutual fund families is available at the site http:/biz.yahoo.com/p/fam/a-b.html.

The Mutual funds are managed by a team of managers (known as the Portfolio Managers) assisted by the Security Analysts who perform investment analysis for them. These mutual fund companies maintain a large staff for sales promotion, marketing of funds, maintenance of records and investor inquiries. The associated costs of analyzing the investments, buying and selling ofsecurities, managing the accounts, and satisfying the reporting requirements arepassed on to the investors in the form of expense ratio. Thus a 1 % expense ratiomeans that the related expense on $1000.00 investment in the fund is $10.00.Since the bulk investment cost is distributed among a large number of invelstors, thecost per investor is less than if the comparable investment was made individually.

9.3 Investment in Mutual Funds

Investing directly in the stocks and bonds requires the investor to pick and evaluate the individual securities from a large universe of stocks and bonds that are available. This requires the expertise and time. Mutual funds provide an alternative to the individual investor where the investor can buy the shares in a mutual fund instead of buying the stocks and/or bonds directly. Here the fund manager makes decisions on buying and selling the specific securities and so the investor is not burdened with that task. Thus investing in a mutual fund is a passive approach to investing.

Since mutual funds mostly consist of a large number of securities, the investor by investing in a mutual fund technically invests in all the securities in the mutual fund ofcourse on the pro rata share of investment in the fund. This provides diversification which reduces the risk as opposed to investing in a single stock because the performance of the mutual fund depends upon the performance of all the securities and their prorata share in the fund. Here the investor also benefits from the expertise of the fund manager as well as the team of security analysts for a very nominal price.

People need to understand the mutual funds because their retirement accounts are mostly invested in them. With a good understanding of the mutual funds, they can allocate their accumulations in proper funds and in suitable proportions depending upon their situation. This also applies to their IRAs which are generally self-directed accounts.

9.4 Types of Mutual Funds

The following are the broad categories of mutual funds in terms of the investment choices:

(a) Stock funds – These funds invest in the stocks of the companies traded on the stock exchanges. There are various kinds of stock mutual funds whose nomenclature is based on the factors such as the capitalization of the companies being large, medium, and small, the characterization of the companies in terms of the growth and value, the companies that pay large dividends, and the domicile of the companies being domestic or international.

The following nomenclature is often used for the stock mutual funds:

Large cap, Medium cap, Small cap and Microcap stock funds,
Growth, Value and Blend stock funds

Capital appreciation funds
Capital opportunity funds
Growth and income funds Blue
chip growth fund
Total return funds
Balanced funds
High yield funds - These funds invest in the stocks of the companies that pay rich dividends.

Sector funds - These funds invest in the stocks of companies in a particular sector such as technology, healthcare, consumer staples, utilities, real estate, etc.

International stock funds - These funds invest most of their money in the companies out of USA. Some international funds concentrate on the specific regions of the world such as the Emerging Markets, Far East, Latin America, Europe, etc. and some even in the specific countries such as China, India, Russia, Turkey, etc.

Global funds – These invest in any part of the world including the US.

Index funds – These funds attempt to mimic the performance of an index such as the S&P 500, Russell 2000, S&P Mid Cap 400, and S&P Small Cap 600, etc.

(b) Bond funds –These mutual funds invest in the different kinds of bonds and the classification is as follows:

Government bond funds
Municipal bond funds
Corporate bond funds
High yield bond funds
International bond funds
Emerging markets bond funds
Inflation linked bond funds
Index bond funds

There is further sub-classification of the bond funds in terms of the duration. The duration refers to the maturity period of the bonds in the fund. Thus there are bond funds of varying durations such as short, medium and long term.

(c) Hybrid funds – These funds are tailored to the specific requirements as indicated below:

(i) Balanced funds - These funds have their portfolios split between the bonds and the stocks.

(ii) Target date funds - These funds are structured to have a portfolio mix suitable for the investors of different age groups to suit their retirement needs.

(iii) Fund of funds - These are the mutual funds that buy other mutual funds to have a portfolio mix with a particular asset allocation.

(d) Money market funds - These funds invest in the short-term and the low- risk securities such as the short-term treasuries and the IOUs of banks. The return from these funds is fairly small but safe. These funds are not subject to market fluctuations. They are used basically for short-term parking of the money which is intended for urgent needs such as the down payment on a home, a major purchase, educational expenses, medical bills, emergencies, etc.

9.5 Open-End versus Closed-End Funds

Open-end funds sell and redeem shares at any time to the shareholders. Thus the total assets of the fund change daily as investors buy and sell shares. The fund shares are bought and redeemed at the net asset value (NAV) which is determined daily at the close of the market taking into account the change in prices of the securities which the fund owns. The shares of the fund can be purchased directly by phone or online if the account with the mutual fund company has liquid funds. Alternatively, the shares can be purchased by mailing funds to the company and the shares will be bought at the net asset value at the close of the day when the funds are received. The shares can also be purchased using the services of a stock broker or financial advisor for a nominal charge. You can also direct the mutual fund company to invest in the fund on a regular basis (such as a fixed amount every month or every quarter) by withdrawing the funds directly from your account. This provides the benefit of compounding.

Close-end mutual funds have the structure of an investment trust. The trust is created by raising funds through an underwriting process. It has a specific set of objectives and has the Board of Directors for oversight. It is managed by the investment manager according to the objectives of the trust. The trust issues a fixed number of shares in its initial public offering. It is these shares only that change hands in the purchase or sale transaction. The fund is thus not subject to the waves of inflows and outflows of funds, unlike an open fund. Since the investment trust does not accept outside money after it starts operating, it works as a closed-end fund. The net asset value (NAV) of the closed end fund depends upon the market prices of the securities as well as the investor demand. If there is greater demand, the fund shares trade at premium (above NAV) and if the demand is lower they trade at discount (below NAV). This investment feature creates an additional level of volatility in a closed-end fund which investors may capitalize on by buying the shares at discount or selling at premium. Like the stocks of individual companies, closed end fund shares trade on a stock exchange. Thus the only way to buy or redeem shares of a closed end fund is by trading them on the stock exchange and not directly form the funds as in the case of open end funds.

9.6 Load and No-load Mutual Funds

There are many costs involved in running a mutual fund such as the remuneration to the fund manager and the team of analysts, administrative costs associated with record keeping, customer mailings, and maintaining the customer service lines. The funds also incur costs of purchasing and selling the shares of the companies. In order to cover these costs, mutual funds charge management fees which vary roughly from 0.65 to 1.2 %. In addition to this, some funds charge for the distribution of sales material, marketing and advertising which is known as the 12b-1 fees. It is about 0.25%.

The difference between a load and no-load mutual fund is in the upfront

charge. In a no-load fund, you buy and sell shares at the net asset value. In other words, there is no upfront charge. In a load fund, there is an upfront sales load which is intended to reimburse the marketing people such as the brokers, financial advisors, investment company etc. through which the fund shares are sold. The initial sales load could vary from about 4% to 8.5% which is deducted from the funds of the investor before the shares in the fund are bought. Thus the actual investment amount is lower than that paid by the investor in a mutual fund with front load. The mutual fund shares with the front load are often called "A" shares.

Some funds have back-end loads and such shares are called "B" shares. These funds impose a contingent deferred sales charge (CDSC) which is paid at the time of redemption. This charge is generally higher than the front-end load. CDSC generally declines incrementally over time and may disappear in five to eight years. This provides incentive to the investors to stay invested in the fund over a long period of time.

Apart from the "A" and "B" share classes, there is a third share class "C" in the load funds. These funds do not charge a front-end or back-end load but impose a higher ongoing 12b-1 fee. Since this fee is paid each year, the longer the fund is held, the more it hurts. There is a false perception that the load funds are better in performance than the no-load funds. This is not true.

The share classes described above belong to the retail category. Some fund families offer no load institutional share class (often tagged as I or Y shares) as well. The initial investment for such shares is very high, usually $1 million or more.

Most funds impose redemption fees in case the shares in the fund are liquidated before a certain period. This is intended to discourage frequent selling and buying of fund shares with the objective of market timing.

9.7 Mutual Fund Prospectus and Services

The detailed information about the mutual fund is available on the fund's internet site as well as the prospectus. The latter can be obtained by calling the fund company or downloading directly from the company website. The prospectus provides all the important information that an investor needs. It consists of the fund objectives, strategy, management, advisory services, risks, fees, distributions, performance, minimum investment, automatic investing option, minimum holding period, and the procedures for opening a new account, purchasing additional shares, and exchanging or redeeming shares.

As for the services, mutual fund companies try to be very investor friendly. Their customer service answers to the queries of prospective investors, mails the prospectus and the application material if needed. The mutual fund companies provide the automatic investing service facility which involves withdrawing the funds from the investor's checking, savings or money market account to make purchases of the fund shares at fixed intervals. This strategy enables the investor to benefit from dollar cost averaging which tends to average out the cost of shares over an extended period of time. This is so because it enables the investor to purchase more shares of the fund in the down market than in the up market for the same amount of money.

Another service provided is the automatic reinvestment of dividends in which the dividends and distributions paid by the fund are directly invested in additional shares of the mutual fund. The companies also provide the facility to let the investor transfer funds between different mutual funds in the same company by a simple phone call. With the same ease, the shares of the fund can also be redeemed.

An additional service which is helpful to the retirees is to set up a plan for the systematic withdrawal of funds in which a specified sum of money realized from the redemption of fund shares at regular intervals is mailed to the investor or credited to his/her bank account. The funds also provide the flexibility of setting up various kinds of tax-deferred accounts such as IRAs, Keoghs, and 401(K)s.

9.8 Risk Parameters

The following are the risk parameters used to signify the risk associated with a mutual fund. These are useful in the selection of a mutual fund to suit the investor's risk profile.

Beta – It provides a measure of the expected variation in the fund price with respect to the market index mimicking the fund. A fund with a beta equal to 1 is expected to go up or down in the same proportion as the market index. On the same lines, a fund with beta greater than 1 will go up or down more than the market index and vice versa. Beta thus provides a measure of the volatility of the fund with respect to the corresponding index.

R-squared - It reflects the percentage of fund's price movement that is explained by the movement in its benchmark index. It ranges from zero to 100%.

Alpha – It measures the difference between a fund's actual return relative to its performance given by beta. A positive alpha figure indicates that the fund has performed better than its beta would indicate. Similarly a negative alpha indicates than the fund has performed worse than its beta.

Standard deviation - It is the statistical measure of the variability of a fund's return with respect to its average annual return. For example, if a fund has an annual average return of 10% and the standard deviation of 15%, then two- thirds of the time the fund's annual return would be expected to fall between (10 – 15) = -5% and (10 + 15) = 25%.

Sharpe ratio - It measures the excess return per unit of total risk. It signifies that the higher a fund's Sharpe ratio, the better its return has been relative to the amount of risk it has taken. Thus if there are two funds with the same performance, the one with a higher Sharpe ratio is better because it took less risk to achieve that performance.

9.9 Categories of Mutual Funds

The categorization often used for domestic stock mutual funds puts them in nine categories as shown in Table 9.1. Here the top row represents large-cap stocks with value, value-growth blend, and growth characteristics. The middle row represents the mid-cap stocks and the bottom row the small-cap stocks with the same three characteristics. Alternatively, the first column represents the value stocks, the second column the blend of value and growth, and the third column the growth stocks. This kind of categorization is helpful in building a diversified investment portfolio of mutual funds. This is so because an investor needs to have funds from more than one category to provide diversification in terms of the capitalization and value versus growth.

Table 9.1 Grid showing nine categories of mutual funds.

Large-cap value	Large-cap blend	Large-cap growth
Mid-cap value	Mid-cap blend	Mid-cap growth
Small-cap value	Small-cap blend	Small-cap growth

Further diversification may be provided by adding to the portfolio the international funds, emerging market funds, sector funds, and bond funds.

9.10 Mutual Fund Ratings

The major rating services for mutual funds use different processes and criteria in assigning their ratings. Ratings are useful for the investors in screening mutual funds while searching for a fund to buy. The most prominent rating agencies are Morningstar, Inc., Lipper and S&P Capital IQ.

· Morningstar

It uses a dual rating system: Star ratings and Analyst ratings. The star-rating system is based on the past performance and is upgraded monthly. It assigns star ratings on a scale of one to five, with five stars being the top rating. Within each fund category, the top 10% of funds receive five-star rating and the bottom 10% of funds receive one-star rating. Of the remainder, 22.5% are assigned four stars, 35% three stars and 22.5% two stars, as shown in Table 9.2. The rating considers the historical performance across three time periods: three-years, five-years and 10-years.

Table 9.2 Morningstar ranking of mutual funds.

No. of stars (*)	Percentile Rank	Rating
5	Top 10%	High
4	Next 22.5%	Above average
3	Middle 35%	Average
2	Next 22.5%	Below average
1	Bottom 10%	Low

The Analyst Ratings are based on the assessment of Analysts for future fund performance. These are assigned Gold, Silver, Bronze, Neutral and Negative in the decreasing order of fund performance. These ratings take into account the tenure and experience of the people managing the fund, stewardship of capital and transparent goals, communication with investors, the clarity and consistency of the process used to generate returns, and the fees charged by the fund.

· Lipper

The rating system by Lipper analyzes the funds on the following criteria: total and consistent return, preservation of capital, tax efficiency and expense ratio. The effective return is a risk-adjusted return measure that looks back over different holding periods (3-year, 5-year, 10-year and lifetime). In each category, the top 20% of funds are named as Lipper Leaders. The next 20% get the rating of four, the middle 20% are rated three, the next 20% are rated two, and the lowest 20% rated as one.

- (c) S&P Capital IQ

Here the ratings are determined using a proprietary methodology based on the funds' underlying holdings. The criterion used is based on the fund type, for example fixed-income funds have different criteria than the equity funds. This rating service provides reports that highlight the funds' portfolio, style, composition, performance and top holdings. The agency bases the risk analysis on the mutual fund's holdings and prior track record. It rates the funds on a scale of one star to five stars, 5 being on the top and 1 on the bottom. The funds with less than three years tenure are not given a star rating.

Kiplinger's Personal Finance Magazine in its issue of June 2016 recommended a number of domestic and international stock mutual funds for investment. It gave the ratings provided by the three rating agencies discussed above for the recommended funds. It showed that the ratings, which were done independently of each other, were fairly similar for each mutual fund except for minor differences in some cases. Thus the reader is advised to use the rating by anyone of the agencies as a guide in the selection of mutual fund for investment purposes.

9.11 Mutual Fund Information Services

Morningstar FundInvestor is an authoritative publication on mutual funds. It includes Fund Investor 500 which provides recommendations and monthly performance data on the top 500 funds. This is the reference on mutual funds used extensively by the investment community. Another equally important source is the Standard & Poor's publication. Both of these are published many times a year. They summarize the performance of mutual funds over specified periods of time while giving also the fund category, star classification, fees, minimum investment, and other information relevant to the selection of fund for investment.

Another publication is Forbes magazine which has a yearly volume exclusively on mutual funds. Other publications such as the Kiplinger's Personal Finance and Consumer Report also publish mutual fund selections in different categories.

The information on mutual funds is also available on the financial websites such as http://www.morningstar.com/Cover/Funds.aspx and http://finance.yahoo.com/funds. The brokerage websites provide screeners to enable the investor to narrow down the list to a few funds based on the criteria selected from practically any category. The select few funds may then be analyzed based on the individual preferences.

9.12 Guidelines for Stock Mutual Fund Selection

1. Decide the mutual fund category in terms of the domestic vs. international, capitalization (large, medium or small cap), and value vs. growth styles. This selection should be made on the basis of asset allocation in your portfolio. For the sake of this example, we will consider a domestic mid-cap value fund.

2. We will consider a no-load fund because we want all our money to be invested and working for us. This consideration is guided by the fact that there is no evidence that the load funds perform better than the no-load funds.

3. Select three or four funds from the recommended list of funds in the financial publications such as Kiplinger's, Money, Forbes, or your brokerage website. Alternatively pick the funds from the US-News website http://money.usnews.com/funds/mutual-funds/ which provides listing of the ranked mutual funds. The U.S.

News Mutual Fund rankings are based on the ratings from Morningstar, Lipper, Zacks, TheStreet.com, and Standard & Poor's. They provide a look at everything from a fund's track record to the predictions of where it might be headed in the future.

4. Delete the funds which have Instl. Category designation. These are the institutional funds which require a large initial investment (about a million dollars) and so are not suitable for small investors.

5. Applying the criterion of no-load funds, delete the funds with the classification A and B because those are load funds.

6. Delete the funds with 3 stars and less because we are interested in 4 and 5 stars only.

7. Delete the funds with high turnover rates (generally greater than 50%) because high turnover rates contribute to large distributions and so are highly tax-inefficient. Note that as an investor in a mutual fund you share in the capital gains and losses anytime a security in the fund is sold. You share also in the distributions that come from the dividends that the security pays.

8. Delete the funds with high expense ratios, anything greater than 1% is high for domestic funds.

9. Analyze the remaining funds with respect to the following aspects: annualized return for 3-5 years, peer group rank, expenses, risk parameters, etc.

9.13 Selection of a Mutual Fund Using Brokerage Website

The brokerage sites provide tools to enable you to select the funds to suit your criteria. To begin with they provide their own prescreened selections of mutual funds in different categories. In addition to that they provide a general screener which enables you to mark your choices to each category such as large, mid or small cap, growth, value or blend star ratings, fees, performance, and other criteria as discussed in the earlier section. The sites are fairly easy to navigate and the brokerages will be happy to help you if needed. The process will save you time and effort and you will have the funds with your exact choices in no time.

9.14 Bond Mutual Funds

Similar to the stock mutual funds, the bond mutual funds may also be categorized. Table 9.3 shows nine categories of bond mutual funds. Here the horizontal rows represent the high quality, the medium quality and the low quality bonds and the vertical columns correspond to the short duration, the intermediate duration and the long duration bonds. Thus the combination of the bond quality and the bond duration gives nine types of bonds as shown in the grid below.

Table 9.3 Grid showing nine categories of bond funds.

Short duration, high quality	Intermediate duration, high quality	Long duration, high quality
Short duration, medium quality	Intermediate duration, medium quality	Long duration, medium quality
Short duration, low quality	Intermediate duration, low quality	Long duration, low quality

9.15 Examination of a Bond Mutual Fund

For the sake of illustration, we will examine the Dodge & Cox Income mutual fund which has the ticker symbol DODIX. This fund was selected because of the following reasons:

1. As of March 29, 2017 it had the Morningstar Gold rating with 4 stars.
2. The data on the brokerage website said that it was an intermediate

duration, medium quality, domestic bond fund. The rationale for its selection was the duration risk in the current interest rate atmosphere. During the last few years, the interest rates have been very low but are expected to rise soon. The bond prices go down with the increase in interest rate and the longer the bond duration the greater is the downside risk. Considering these factors, this bond with the intermediate duration presented medium risk which was prudent in the current atmosphere. By going with a shorter duration bond, the risk could have been reduced but the yield would be much smaller.

3. The description of the fund said that it was a domestic bond fund with more than 80% exposure in North America. Its total return over the last ten years had been mostly better than the index.

4. The breakdown of the securities in the fund was 6.7% Govt., 49.1% Corporate, 34.6% Securitized, 4% Municipal and 5% cash. Note that most of the bonds were investment grade.

5. The narrative talked about the veteran and well-resourced team of managers, time-tested process, low expenses and an impressive long-term record.

6. It had no sales load, no redemption fees and no administrative fees. It had the management fees of 0.6% which is reasonable.

7. The investment philosophy stated to give preference to the holdings in high quality companies, which are characterized by earnings that are reasonably predictable, have a return on equity that is above average, hold market dominance and have financial strength.

8. The load adjusted returns were more than 6% for a year, 11% for 5 years and about 8% for 10 years which is a good track record.

9. The Fund Manager had good experience with a tenure of more than 10 years.

10. The initial investment was $2,500 and additional investments were $100. These are reasonable amounts for the people in general.

11. The risk parameters for this fund as stated were as follows:

Alpha 0.07
Standard deviation 12.09 for the fund and 11.67 for the category

Sharpe ratio 0.94 for the fund and 0.82-0.97 for the category R-squared 88.82 for the fund and 94.05 for the category

Beta 1.0 for the fund and 1.0-1.74 for the category

These are all reasonable figures.

9.16 How to Buy Mutual Funds

The process in buying the stock mutual fund or the bond mutual fund is the same. The following discussion is, however, targeted to a stock mutual fund.

The first task is to settle down on the choice of fund. There are mutual funds for almost any situation. If you do not have the investment in a mutual fund, start with a large cap value fund. Gradually broaden your investment to include large cap growth fund, medium cap value and medium cap growth

funds, etc. You should then add an international fund. Later you may add a small cap fund. There is no hard and fast rule for this order but this is a rational way to broaden your investment.

The first task is to settle down on the choice of fund. There are mutual funds for almost any situation. If you do not have investment in any kind of mutual fund, start with a large cap value fund. Gradually broaden your investment to include large cap growth fund, medium cap value and medium cap growth

funds, etc. You should then add an international fund. Later you may add a small cap fund. There is no hard and fast rule for this order, but this is a rational way to broaden your investment.

Next select a no-load mutual fund. There are many good funds from reputable companies. Some of these companies with an assortment of mutual funds are the Vanguard Group, Fidelity Investments, T. Rowe Price, TIAA- CREF, Oakmark, Artisan, Harbor, USAA, Dodge & Cox, Invesco, Pimco, etc. Avoid the Adviser Funds such as those sold by Fidelity. This is the family of load funds sold through investment sales people and so carry higher sales load to compensate them. Similarly avoid the A and B class shares of any mutual fund because these are the share classes with front or backend loads. Vanguard is known for one of the lowest management fees but the fees charged by the other companies listed above are also reasonable.

Make the choice of the fund by following the guidelines discussed in this chapter by paying attention to the fund objectives, strategy, management, advisory services, risks, fees, distributions, performance, minimum investment, etc. Pay attention to the performance of the fund against its closest bench mark over the last few years. All of this information is given in the prospectus.

Do not buy through the brokers or the investment advisors because they sell only the load funds. Do not buy the arguments from investment professionals such as the following:

1. We get paid by the mutual fund company.
2. Load funds are better than no-load funds.
3. No-load funds have higher fees.

Buy shares directly from the mutual fund company and not through a discount broker. The drawback in buying the shares from a discount broker is that you have to pay the transaction fees which can range from about $15 to $50. Download the application form from the company website. Fill in the form and attach a check for the amount to invest and mail the papers to the company. If in doubt, call at the phone number given in the prospectus for any clarification. This is all it takes.

9.17 Summary

1. Mutual funds pool money from a large number of investors and invest it in the stocks, bonds and other assets. If the money is invested in stocks, it is called a stock mutual fund. If invested in bonds, it is a bond mutual fund. If invested in stocks and bonds both, it is called a hybrid mutual fund.

2. Depending upon the capitalization of stocks, a mutual fund may be a small cap, medium cap or large cap mutual fund. Depending upon the nature of stocks in terms of the value and growth, the mutual fund may be a value fund or growth fund.

3. Depending upon the nationality of stocks, a mutual fund may be an international fund, emerging market fund or a specific country or region fund.

4. An index mutual fund is structured on the pattern of the particular index representing the same stocks as in the index and in about the same proportions.

5. Mutual funds are managed by a team of analysts working under a portfolio manager. They belong normally to a big mutual fund company which has a number of funds in different categories.

6. Mutual funds charge fees to cover the management and analyst expenses. Some of them charge an extra fees of $1/4 - 1/2\%$ called the 12(b) fees to maintain the records and for customer inquiries.

7. There are two types of mutual funds: open-end and closed-end. Open-end mutual funds redeem shares any time to shareholders at the net asset value which is calculated when the market closes. Closed end mutual funds have the structure of a trust and have a fixed number of shares. Once started, the trust does not accept outside money. Here the net asset value depends upon the market prices of the securities in the fund as well as the demand. So they may trade at premium or discount.

8. Mutual funds may be load or no-load. Load funds charge customers an initial fees to get in the fund.

9. Mutual funds have the risk parameters such as alpha, beta, sharpe ratio, standard deviation etc. which are useful in the selection for investment.

10. The funds are assigned ratings by Morningstar, Lipper and S&P Global. These may be used in the selection of mutual funds.

Suggested Action Items

Analyze and select a Large Cap Value fund and a Small Cap Growth fund from anyone of the following major mutual fund companies: Fidelity, T. Rowe Price and Vanguard. Open the account and invest at least the minimum amount in any two funds. Monitor their prices with changes in the stock market prices.

Chapter 10

Investment in Exchange Traded Funds

10.1 Introduction

This chapter deals with the exchange-traded funds, commonly known as the ETFs. They are used generally to track the performance of a specific market segment. They are also used to track the prices of commodities and various other assets. There are ETFs representing different sectors of the market but they are not as actively managed as the mutual funds. They trade on the stock exchanges just like stocks using the same techniques such as shorting, buying on margin, or using stop-loss orders to sell them. Their prices fluctuate throughout the trading day when the market is open.

10.2 Exchange Traded Funds

The exchange-traded funds (commonly known as ETFs) were introduced in 1993 as a way to provide access to passive indexed funds to individual investors. Since their inception the ETFs have exploded in popularity. The share of the funds in mutual funds has been decreasing while that of the ETFs increasing. ETFs resemble the mutual funds in that they have a portfolio of stocks or bonds but unlike mutual funds they trade actively on the stock exchanges. Similar to the mutual funds, ETFs provide diversification and can be tracked in price like that of a stock. The shares of an ETF can be purchased or sold any time the market is open. Their prices fluctuate throughout the trading day just like that of the stocks. The market price of an ETF is governed by the prices of the stocks in the ETF and the supply and demand for its shares. When the demand for the shares of an ETF exceeds

supply, the ETF could trade at a premium to NAV; and when the supply exceeds demand, the ETF could trade at a discount to NAV. In general ETFs do not trade at persistent large premiums or discounts because the market makers create and redeem shares thereby arbitraging any premium or discount. Like the stocks one can short them, buy on margin and even use stop-loss orders to sell them. In this respect, they differ from the open-end mutual funds which are always bought and sold at the NAV that is calculated at the end of the trading day.

The trading commissions for ETFs used to be the same or less as for the stocks but recently the internet brokerages announced to waive them. ETFs have very small expenses compared to the mutual funds because they are not actively managed. Instead ETFs undergo portfolio rebalancing often quarterly or annually. This results in capital gains which are fairly small and this makes them more tax-efficient. The risks in an ETF are the same as that of the group of stocks it is meant to represent.

In addition to the ordinary ETFs, there are leveraged ETFs which are available for most indexes such as the Dow Jones Industrial Average and Nasdaq-100. For example, a leveraged ETF with a 2:1 ratio means that each dollar of invested capital is matched with an additional dollar of invested debt. So if the index returns 1%, the fund will theoretically return 2%. Note that the 2% return is theoretical because the management fees and other costs diminish the full effect of leverage. The 2:1 ratio works in the opposite direction as well which means that if the index drops 1%, the loss would then be 2%. Since the drop is magnified, leverage ETFs are fairly risky.

The roster of ETFs is diverse and ever increasing which helps to build the whole portfolio from them. For example, some are traditional index funds which means that they track the benchmarks that weigh holdings by market value. Some are smart beta ETFs which track a designer index that is built to do better than a particular segment of the market. Some are leveraged ETFs and so on.

Similar to the ETFs there are ETNs. The latter are the structured products that are issued as senior debt notes while ETFs represent a stake in an underlying commodity. When you invest in an ETF, you are investing in a fund that holds the assets it tracks. Those assets may be stocks, bonds, gold or other commodities, or futures contracts. An ETN is more like a bond. It's an unsecured debt note issued by an institution.

The commission rates for trading ETFs have recently been eliminated by internet brokerages just like that of stocks. ETFs have smaller expenses compared to the mutual funds because they are not that actively managed. Instead ETFs undergo portfolio rebalancing often quarterly or annually. This results in capital gains which are fairly small and this makes them more tax-efficient. The risks in an ETF are the same as that of the group of stocks it is meant to represent.

While mutual funds report their holdings on a quarterly or semiannual basis, ETFs disclose their portfolio holdings on a daily basis. This provides ETF investors with a greater degree of financial transparency. The ETF performance and the portfolio composition are a reflection of the underlying index or the basket of securities.

The comparison between the stocks, mutual funds and ETFs is shown in Table 10.1.

Table 10.1 Comparison between stocks, ETFs and mutual funds.

	Stocks	ETFs	Mutual Funds
Continuous trading and pricing throughout the day	Yes	Yes	No
Can be bought on margin	Yes	Yes	No
Can buy/sell options	Yes	Yes	No
Can be actively traded	Yes	Yes	No
Tax efficient	Yes	Yes	Sometimes
Expense ratio	N/A	Typically lower	Typically higher

10.3 ETFS for Market Indexes

The stock market index applies to a section of the stock market. It is computed from the prices of selected stocks and is typically a weighted average. Stock market indices may be classified in many ways such as regions like America, Europe, Asia, India, Japan, Asia Pacific, Developed Europe, etc. The concept is also extended more broadly to include the stocks traded on different exchanges such as New York Stock Exchange, American Stock Exchange, NASDQ, etc. and various sectors such as technology, biotechnology, real estate, etc. All the major stock indexes have ETFs based on them. Table 10.2 gives the ETF ticker symbols for popular market indexes.

Table 10.2 ETF Ticker symbols for market indexes.

Index	Ticker Symbol	Description
Dow Jones Industrial Average	DJIA	Diamonds Trust - a benchmark of 30 blue-chip stocks
Standard & Poor's 500	SPY IVV	Performance of 500 large cap companies Same as above but from a different source
Standard & Poor's 400	MDY	Performance of Mid-Cap 400 companies
NASDQ 100	QQQ	Technology benchmark based on 100 large companies
Russell 2000	IWM	The benchmark based on 2000 mid and small cap companies
Small Cap 600	IJR	The benchmark based on 600 small cap companies
SPDR DJ Wilshire	TMW	Broad market index based on 5000 companies
Total Stock Market	VTI	Same as above but from a different company
MSCI EAFE	EFA	Non-US large cap companies, no emerging markets
Lehman Aggregate Bond	AGG	Performance of Govt. and highly-rated corporate bonds

10.4 ETFS for Market Sectors

Similar to the market indexes, there are ETFs for different sectors of the market, such as large US companies, small companies, real estate investment

trusts (REITs), international stocks, bonds, commodities and even currencies. This makes possible for an investor to participate in the whole sector of the market with just ETFs. Since many investment companies have introduced their own ETFs mirroring the performance of the same sectors, the choices in each category are sometimes multiple. Table 10.3 gives the ticker symbols for SPDR ETFs representing the various sectors.

Table 10.3 SPDR ETF symbols for various market sectors.

SPDR ETF Symbols	Sector name with examples
XLY	Consumer discretionary – restaurants, transportation, home repair items, recreation
XLP	Consumer staples – items of daily needs
XLE	Energy – companies dealing with oil exploration and refining, wind energy, ethanol
XLF	Financial – banks, credit cards, financial services
XLV	Health care – drug and pharmaceutical companies, nursing homes, hospitals
XLI	Industrial – machinery, aircrafts, railroads
XLB	Materials – chemicals, mining, industrial materials, precious metals
XLK	Technology – computers, chips, software, internet
XLU	Utilities – utility companies dealing with the generation and distribution of electricity and gas
XLRE	Real estate

10.5 ETF Families

Many financial companies have introduced their own ETFs. However, the vast majority of investment dollars are under the control of just a handful of ETF families. Nearly one out of every two ETF dollars is placed with an iShares fund. The latter is owned by the BlackRock family. SPDR State Street Global Advisors ranks second and Vanguard ranks third among the fund families in terms of the ETF assets. Combined, more than 80% of all ETF dollars are invested with these three fund families. Table 10.4 provides the listing of 14 largest ETFs which can be used for all kinds of markets.

Table 10.4 List of 14 largest ETFs

SPDR S&P 500 (SPY)
iShares Core S&P 500 (IVV)
iShares MSCI EAFE (EFA)
Vanguard Emerging Markets Stock Idx ETF (VWO)
Vanguard Total Stock Market ETF (VTI)
PowerShares QQQ (QQQ)
iShares MSCI Emerging Markets (EEM)
SPDR Gold Shares (GLD)
iShares Russell 2000 (IWM)
Vanguard REIT Index ETF (VNQ)
iShares Russell 1000 Growth (IWF)
iShares Core S&P Mid-Cap (IJH)
Vanguard FTSE Developed Markets ETF (VEA)
iShares Russell 1000 Value (IWD)

10.6 Leveraged and Inverse Exchange Traded Funds

The leveraged ETFs were created to magnify the move of a specific index, such as the Standard and Poor's (S&P) 500 stock index, by many times. So for a 1 percent increase in the S&P 500 index, a double-leveraged S&P 500 ETF is supposed to increase by 2 percent, a triple-leveraged S&P 500 ETF to increase by 3 percent and so on. The inverse ETFs are intended to move in the direction opposite to that of a given index. For example, an inverse S&P 500 ETF is supposed to increase by 1 percent for a 1 percent drop in the S&P 500 index. Thus one could make money even when the market is falling.

The above ETFs have been found to be very risky over extended time periods. As such the Financial Industry Regulatory Authority (FINRA), which is the regulator of the securities firms, has issued the warning that leveraged and inverse ETFs are not suitable for retail investors. The financial advisors are thus not typically allowed to recommend these ETFs to their clients. These are basically the gambling instruments for day traders and so retail investors are advised not to deal with them at all.

10.7 Smart-Beta ETFs

Another variation of the ETFs is the smart beta version. These ETFs use various fundamental screens searching for the factors like sales, earnings, book value, dividends and cash flows etc. to create or improve upon the traditional ETFs. The idea is that by focusing on these factors the new smart- beta ETFs will outperform the market cap weighted funds like the SPDR S&P 500 ETF (SPY). Because of the large screen choices, there are literally hundreds of such ETFs which makes it difficult to know which smart beta ETF is actually smart for your portfolio. The examples of such funds are the following:

1. PowerShares FTSE RAFI US 1000 ETF (Ticker symbol: PRF) – It uses screens targeting the size, book value, sales and dividends across the entire US stock market. It assigns each a score based on these screens and weighs them according to that score rather than by the market cap. The result is that it provides a make-up completely different from the traditional Russell 1000 index.

2. Goldman Sachs ActiveBeta U.S. Large Cap Equity ETF (Ticker symbol: GSLC) - This includes screening for the value of a stock, momentum, quality and volatility. The result is that it gives the best US large cap stocks which are cheap and have quality earnings with plenty of price action.

3. FlexShares Credit-Scored US Corp Bond ETF (Ticker symbol: SKOR) – This is the example of a smart-beta bond ETF. The idea here is that a bond ETF too can benefit from the focus on fundamentals. The ETF scores intermediate corporate bonds on various factors such as the duration, credit spreads/value and other characteristics of a bond. Using a proprietary model for credit, the smart-beta ETF removes the bonds with credit issues and loads up on those that are good values.

10.8 Bond ETFS

Like stock ETFs, bond ETFs offer broadly diversified exposure to a segment of the bond market in a single investment. They trade on the stock exchange and so can be bought and sold anytime the exchange is open. They serve as a lower-cost alternative to the individual bonds. They may track broad indexes of the different kinds of bonds such as the investment-grade bonds, corporate bonds, municipal bonds, high yield bonds and even foreign bonds. There are ETFs which hold Treasury Inflation-Protected Securities (TIPS), government bonds and municipal bonds. In addition to these, there are Target maturity bond ETFs which hold bonds maturing in the same year.

While the investor in an individual bond is paid back the face value at maturity, this is not the case with ETFs because they do not mature. As such the bond ETF investor has to sell the ETF at prevailing price in order to cash out. The bond ETFs pay dividends monthly or quarterly and capital gains at year end just like in the case of stocks or stock ETFs. The ETFs carry the same risk as the bonds which are the interest rate risk, credit risk and liquidity risk. The price of the bond ETF fluctuates based on the value of the bonds in the index.

10.9 Country or Region-Specific ETFs

Like the domestic ETFs, we have the ETFs for investing in the foreign markets including the specific foreign countries. For example, there are ETFs for the countries such as China, India, Korea, Japan, Canada, and Russia as well as the specific regions such as Europe, Far-East, Latin America, emerging markets, developed markets and the like.

For the sake of discussion, let us say that we are interested in investing in the emerging markets. Considering that the GDP of India has been growing at the rate of 6 - 8% per year, the investment in the Indian stock market looks attractive. An ETF could be a reasonable choice because it would provide diversification as well as the investment in major companies with minimal effort. Table 10.5 gives six India ETFs where INP and INDY are for the stock market indexes, INR and ICN for the currencies, and PIN and EPI for Indian equities from two different sponsors.

Table 10.5 ETFs for the investment in India.

ETF Name	Ticker	Asset Class	Sponsor
iPath MSCI India Index ETN	INP	Equities	iPath
iShares S&P India Nifty 50 Index Fund	INDY	Equities	iShares
Market Vectors Indian Rupee-USD ETN	INR	Currencies	Morgan Stanley
PowerShares India Portfolio	PIN	Equities	PowerShares
WisdomTree India Earnings Fund	EPI	Equities	WisdomTree
WisdomTree Dreyfus Indian Rupee	ICN	Currencies	WisdomTree

10.10 Funds of Funds ETFs

While a regular ETF holds a basket of securities, an ETF fund of funds owns a basket of other ETFs. They can be divided into two categories such as those focused on asset allocation and those focused on sectors or themes. The asset allocation ETF holds a mixture of ETFs focused on stocks, bonds and other assets. For example, iShares Core Moderate Allocation ETF (AOM) is about 54% bonds and 39% stocks while iShares Core Aggressive Allocation ETF (AOA) has about 19% bonds and 79% stocks. There is another fund of funds Global X Thematic Growth ETF which is comprised of the funds from artificial intelligence and e-commerce themes. The idea here is that one fund of fund ETF may provide diversification thereby avoiding the need of many ETFs.

10.11 Investment in an ETF

The same type of information as described for the mutual funds in Chapter 9 is available for the ETFs as well on the financial websites as well as the company website. The following is an overview of the type of information available:

> · Strategy of the ETF ·
> Star rating
>
> · NAV, Premium/ Discount, Yield, Total assets, Expense ratio, Minimum investment amount
> · Fund Manager and tenure ·
> Risk and Return profile
> · Top sectors and holdings
> · Returns for different periods, Yearly price variation chart
> · Listing of companies and % investments ·
> Risk parameters

With the same type of information as for the mutual funds, the ETF selection process is also the same as already covered for the mutual funds in Chapter 9.

Unlike the mutual fund where you place order with a mutual fund company, you place order for the ETF on the internet Brokerage site just like for any stock discussed above.

10.12 Summary

1. The exchange traded funds, commonly known as the ETFs, are used to track the performance of market indexes as well as the basket of securities in different segments.
2. ETFs trade on the stock exchanges like stocks and so can be bought and sold any time the stock exchanges are open.
3. They may trade sometimes at premium or discount depending upon the supply and demand imbalance.
4. In addition to the normal ETFs, there are leveraged and inverse ETFs which accentuate the effect of market swings.
5. In addition to the stock ETFs, there are ETFs for corporate and municipal bonds and treasury inflation protected securities as well.
6. Unlike mutual funds, ETFs are not actively managed.

Suggested Action Items

Look into the ETFs for the healthcare sector and study the differences in them. Consider a small investment in the ETF of your choice for maximum appreciation potential.

Chapter 11

Asset Allocation, Diversification and Portfolio Rebalancing

11.1 Introduction

This chapter introduces the concept of asset allocation in a portfolio. The latter is comprised of the different types of assets which may be correlated or non-correlated. Utilizing this variance in correlation, it is possible to develop the portfolios which ensure maximum return with minimum risk. The risk is further reduced by the selection of non-correlated securities in each asset class. Asset allocation is guided by the factors such as the present and future wealth of the investor, his/ her age, and time for the money to grow, and the risk tolerance. The strategies for asset allocation are discussed and the need for diversification emphasized. Some asset allocation guidelines have been provided.

11.2 Asset Classes and their Volatility

An asset class is a broad category of related securities. Broadly speaking, the asset classes commonly used for asset allocation include equities (stocks), bonds, and cash or cash equivalents. Some investors, mostly wealthy, include also the real estate, precious metals and other commodities as well as the private equity. We will, however, limit our discussion to the common asset classes namely equities, bonds and cash equivalents.

As for the stocks, these include individual stocks, stock mutual funds and exchange traded funds. The stocks could vary in terms of the capitalization, value versus growth, sector, and domestic versus international. They have historically provided the highest returns but are volatile and this makes them risky. Owning the stocks is necessary to get the expected return needed to accumulate the funds for retirement.

Many investors learned how risky the stocks could be when in the year 2008 they fell 50% from their previous highs.Over time, the stock prices follow roughly the trend of the economy, which is to grow. But stock prices can stagnate or decline for extended periods. This is why having a supplemental allocation of bonds to the base stock portfolio is a necessary element of the asset allocation.

As for the bonds, these could include all kinds of bonds and bond mutual funds. Compared to the stocks, bonds and bond mutual funds with the exception of high yield bonds are less volatile but their returns are more modest too. The lower volatility makes bonds the favorite choice of investment for the retired people. One the other hand, high-yield bonds (commonly known as the junk bonds) are fairly volatile and provide high return similar to that of the stocks.

While referring to the cash and cash equivalents, people invest in the certificates of deposit, savings bonds, treasury bills, treasury inflation protected securities, money market funds, etc. These investments are safer compared to the stocks and bonds but offer lower returns. The likelihood of losing money from such investments is fairly small because many of these are backed by the US Government Treasury. As such the main risk here is the inflation risk. This is the risk that inflation will outpace and erode investment returns from these over time.

Practically speaking, all investments involve some degree of risk. The reward for taking risk is the potential for a greater investment return. The longer the time horizon, the more risk one can take by investing in stocks and high-yield bonds. On the other hand, investing solely in the cash investments and short- term bonds is appropriate for the short-term financial goals.

11.3 Sub-Asset Classes

In each of the asset classes mentioned above, there are sub-asset classes. For example, in the category of stocks we have large-cap, mid-cap and small-cap stocks, with value and growth types in each category, domestic and international stocks, and emerging market stocks. In the category of bonds, there are municipal bonds, corporate bonds and treasury bonds, with the first two in investment grade or junk category. Each of these carries a risk of its own as in Table 11.1. Some of these assets move in tandem and some against, to varying amounts, depending upon the changes in market condition.

Table 11.1 Listing of various assets in increasing order of risk.

No	Name of asset	Risk and return potential
1	Money market or Government treasuries	Lowest risk of any asset class, lowest return too
2	Investment grade corporate bonds	Higher risk and higher return than in 1 above
3	Large cap equities	Higher risk and higher return than in 2 above
4	Midcap equities	Higher risk and higher return than in 3 above
5	Small cap equities	Higher risk and higher return than in 4 above

This difference in the direction and the degree of movement makes theoretically possible to build an ideal portfolio which will give the maximum return with minimum risk. In this respect, the Markowitz portfolio model is often cited but it is too complex to use in a practical sense. As such we are concerned here only with the concept of reducing risk by combining these asset classes while aiming for the maximum return within this constraint. Along with this, we will make use of another concept which is known as diversification. This says that by selecting a relatively large number of securities randomly the risk is greatly reduced, as shown in Table 11.2. The random selection of securities implies that the investment characteristics such as the expected return and the industry classification are not being considered. It should be noted that a two-stock portfolio has the reduced risk of 0.76 compared to 1 for a single-stock portfolio. That amounts to a reduction of 24%. With 4 stocks the risk is reduced by 40% and a portfolio of 10 stocks will have even lower risk. This a very important observation which says that one should avoid having a single stock portfolio. Furthermore, the risk is considerably reduced by adding a few more stocks to the portfolio. Another point to note is that as the number of stocks becomes larger, the effect in terms of the reduction of risk becomes smaller.

In practice, the 10 to 20 stock portfolio is considered ideal from the consideration of risk. Furthermore, the securities should be non-correlated which means that they do not move in cohesion with the changes in economic conditions and fiscal policy.

Table 11.2 Expected risk of portfolios.

No of stocks in portfolio	Portfolio risk/ Risk of a single stock
1	1.0
2	0.76
4	0.60
10	0.49
20	0.44

11.4 Asset Allocation

The term asset allocation refers to the allocation of portfolio funds to different classes of asset categories with the investment returns that move up and down differently under different market conditions. It has been found historically that the returns of the three major classes of assets, namely stocks, bonds and cash equivalents, do not always move up and down at the same time. In other words, the market condition that makes one asset class do better often makes other asset classes do poorer and vice versa. For example, the stocks do better in a thriving economy but the bonds do poorly because of the likelihood of higher interest rates needed to constrain inflation in the heated economy. Similarly the economy which is good for high bond returns is not necessarily good for high stock returns. Thus, by investing in both the stocks and the bonds together, the likelihood of the return on investment is smoother because while one loses money the other gains it.

Thus the key reason for asset allocation is to help the investor to reduce risk from volatile stocks (which are expected to provide higher return) by combining them with more stable asset classes such as the bonds and the fixed-income assets. The factors to consider in making the asset allocation decision include the investor's return requirements, risk tolerance and the time horizon.

The first item has to do with the anticipated future needs of the person as in retirement. The risk tolerance is related to the present wealth situation because a person with enough funds for retirement living can afford to take greater risk. On the other hand, a person with limited funds cannot take too much risk because there would not be much left to depend on in case the losses occur. The time horizon plays a very big role because the risk from investing in risky assets such as stocks is greatly reduced given enough time. Thus a greater allocation to stocks becomes a possibility with longer times.

The basic question in asset allocation is how much of the portfolio be put in stocks, how much in bonds, and how much in cash equivalents. The guiding principle in deciding this allocation is that a young person in prime earning years is going to need access to the money decades later. So a high allocation to stocks will be in order because over extended times one can recoup losses if that should occur. As we age, the time to recover losses decreases, this would suggest that we reduce the stock allocation and increase the bond allocation. For needs such as the emergencies, down payment on a home, car purchase etc., some allocation to the cash and cash equivalents will also be desirable. Based on these guidelines, various asset allocation ideas have been proposed. For example, the legendary investor Benjamin Graham suggested as a fundamental guiding rule that an investor should have never less than 25% in bonds or more than 75% of funds in common stocks, with a consequence inverse range of 75% to 25% in bonds. Another great investor John Bogle recommended that the bond

contribution should equal roughly the age of the investor. For instance, at age 45 about 45% of the portfolio should be allocated to high-quality bonds. The age-based asset allocation guideline is the most common. It says that the allocation to stocks should be reduced as the person approaches the retirement age and the remainder funds be invested in safer investments such as the bonds and cash instruments.

It should be realized that asset allocation is a personal decision. It should be decided within the suggested guidelines in view of the personal requirements. It is impossible to devise an asset allocation which in retrospect would be the best asset allocation. William J. Bernstein in his book "The Four Pillars of Investing" McGraw Hill, said "In short, during the next 20 or 30 years, there will be a single, best allocation that in retrospect we will have wished we have owned. The only problem is that we haven't a clue what that portfolio will be.

So, the safest course is to own as many asset classes as you can; that way you can be sure of avoiding the catastrophe of holding a portfolio concentrated in the worst ones."

Asset allocation will differ with varying financial goals. For example, if investing for a long-term goal such as retirement, it is necessary to invest in stocks because they provide higher returns with acceptable volatility over long periods. If saving money for the college education of a child about 15 years later, a mixture of stocks and bonds would be the choice. Here the proportion of stocks and bonds in the portfolio would vary depending upon the time when money will be needed. As a general rule, the longer the time period, the greater should be the proportion of stocks and vice versa. The risk of course is that if there is too much risk or too little risk in the portfolio, there may not be enough money for the intended goal. It should thus be noted that the success depends upon the proper asset allocation.

The financial advisors and the financial companies emphasize strongly the need for asset allocation to their clients. Many of them have computer programs to work out the asset allocation for their clients based on different criteria. For example, the Iowa Public Employees Retirement System (https://www.ipers.org/) has Asset Allocation Calculator on its website. It uses as its input the employee age, current assets, savings per year, marginal tax rate, income required and the risk tolerance. With the proper input, it gives the asset allocation in terms of the stocks, bonds and cash assets. For example, for a person of age 45 years, current assets of $100,000, savings per year of $5,000, income required before retirement zero, marginal tax rate of 28%, risk tolerance of 5 on a scale of 10, and moderate economic outlook, it gave the suggested asset allocation of 65% stocks, 15% bonds and 20% cash. When the age was changed to 65 years, the suggested asset allocation changed to 46% stocks, 22% bonds and 32% cash. Note that with the increase in age, the proportion of stocks decreased while those of the bonds and the cash increased.

From the above discussion, it should be realized that the concept of asset allocation is simple but it is impossible to devise one that is going to be the best in hindsight. There are many internet sources of information on asset allocation available. Many of these are from the leading financial companies such as www.vanguard.com, www.troweprice.com, www.schwab.com and www.tdameritrade.com. These sites provide valuable information on the subject of asset allocation. They prompt you to answer a few questions related to your situation of the time and risk, etc. Based on the input, they suggest the asset allocation for you.

11.5 Asset Allocation Strategies

Asset allocation is a dynamic process and may be changed depending upon the changing circumstances. The following strategies are used to change the asset allocation:

1. Strategic Asset Allocation – This uses an asset mix using the proportional combination of assets based on the expected rates of return for each asset class. For example, if stocks have historically returned 10% per year and bonds 5% per year, a mix of 50% stocks and 50% bonds would be expected to return 7.5% per year. With the change in values of the assets, the drift in the initial mix will occur but no adjustment is made to account for this change.

2. Constant-Weighting Asset Allocation – Here, instead of the percentage allocation as above, the weighting of the assets is kept constant by balancing when any one asset class moves more than 5% from its original value.

3. Tactical Asset Allocation – Here the change in asset mix is made based on the expected returns from stocks, bonds and other assets. It is thus a market timing approach to portfolio management intended to increase the exposure to a particular asset class when its performance is expected to be good and decrease the exposure when performance is expected to be poor.

4. Dynamic Asset Allocation – Here the mix of assets is adjusted constantly as the markets rise and fall and as the economy strengthens or weakens. It means that the assets expected to decline are sold and those expected to appreciate are bought.

5. Insured Asset Allocation – Here a base portfolio value is established below which the portfolio value is not allowed to drop. This uses active management to increase the value of the portfolio as long as the portfolio value is above the minimum

value established. If the portfolio value drops below the minimum established, the portfolio is then invested in risk-free assets such as the cash instruments so that further drop in the value does not occur.

6. Integrated Asset Allocation – It includes the strategies accounting not only for the expectations but also for the actual changes in capital markets and the risk tolerance.

11.6 Model Portfolios

The following are some of the model portfolios ranging from conservative to very aggressive. They satisfy a particular level of investor risk tolerance and so are presented here only as a guideline. They include three kinds of assets: stocks, bonds and cash equivalents.

(a) Conservative Portfolio or Capital Preservation Portfolio – Its main goal is to protect the principal value of the portfolio (which is the money originally invested). Here a large percentage of the portfolio is allocated to lower-risk securities such as the fixed-income and money market securities. Some exposure to high-quality blue chip stocks is recommended to help offset the inflation. Alternatively the equity portion may be invested in an index fund.

15 – 20 % equities, 70 – 75 % fixed income securities, 5 – 15 % cash and cash equivalents

(b) Moderately Conservative Portfolio or Current Income Portfolio – It is for the investors who want to preserve a large portion of the portfolio's total value, but are willing to take on a higher amount of risk to get some inflation protection. The equity portion here may be invested in high dividend stocks.

35 – 40 % equities, 55 – 60 % fixed income securities, 5 – 10 % cash and cash equivalents

(c) Moderately Aggressive Portfolio or Balanced Portfolio – Here the asset allocation is divided almost equally between the fixed-income securities and the equities so as to provide a balance of growth and income. This portfolio is the best for investors with a medium level of risk tolerance and with a time horizon of more than five years.

50 – 55 % equities, 35 – 40 % fixed income securities, 5 – 10 % cash and cash equivalents

(d) Aggressive Portfolio – This consists of the equities mainly and so fluctuates in value with the market conditions. The goal here is the long- term growth of capital. In order to provide some diversification, investors may add some fixed-income securities.

65 – 70 % equities, 20 – 25 % fixed income securities, 5 – 10 % cash and cash equivalents

(e) Very Aggressive Portfolios – It consists almost entirely of the equities. The main goal here is the aggressive growth of capital over a long time horizon. Such portfolios carry a considerable amount of risk and their value fluctuates widely in the short term.

80 – 100 % equities, 0 – 10 % fixed income securities, 0 – 10 % cash and cash equivalents

The portfolios described above offer only a loose guideline. Within this framework, one can modify the proportions to suit the individual investment needs. For example, one may refine these portfolios by selecting the subclasses of stocks. For the bond portion, one can invest in different kinds of bonds with differing returns and maturities. Similarly the cash and cash equivalents may be placed in instruments with different amounts of returns and safety.

11.7 Asset Correlation

It refers to the relationship between the directions of movement of two or more assets with the changing market conditions. If the assets move up and down together, they are said to have positive correlation. If they move inversely to each other, they are said to have negative correlation. If there is no relationship between the movements of assets, they are said to have zero correlation. Combining multiple assets with no correlation leads to an ideal diversified portfolio because the volatility (or risk) of the portfolio would be minimized. In practice, the majority of assets have some correlation and that too in a positive way. Thus building a portfolio with the right mixture of assets is difficult. Not only this but also the correlations are dynamic which means that they tend to change with time. This means that an ideally non- correlated portfolio today may become partially correlated with time. In practice, cash is the only asset with zero correlation with other assets and so it serves as an ideal asset to preserve capital in bear markets.

The concept of asset correlation is important in building a portfolio with low volatility. According to this concept, the volatility of the portfolio can be reduced by combining assets with low correlation or negative correlation. This leads to the idea of building a diversified portfolio of stocks and bonds or stocks, bonds and treasury securities which is often done in practice.

11.8 Diversification

It refers to the old time saying "Don't put all your eggs in one basket". In the context of portfolio, it implies the strategy which involves spreading your money among various investments. The idea here is that if one investment loses money, the other will wholly or partially make it up. A diversified portfolio should be diversified at two levels: between asset categories and within asset categories. The first refers to the diversification between asset classes as covered in section 11.2. The second refers to the diversification in each of the sub-assets covered in section 11.3. For example, if we consider the sub-asset category of large cap stocks, we should be having stocks of different companies in non-correlated or partially non-correlated businesses.

The same applies to mid-cap and small-cap stock categories. The problem with this approach is that the number of companies needed to invest may become too large. In that case, some diversification may be achieved by investing in exchange traded funds (ETFs), mutual funds (domestic and international) or stock market index funds. It should be noted that some ETFs and mutual funds which invest in a specific industry sector may not provide the desired diversification.

For some people who are not comfortable with the selection of individual stocks or stock funds, an alternative product known as the lifecycle fund is being offered. This is a diversified mutual fund which adjusts to the more conservative mix of investments with time. These funds are typically targeted to individuals in retirement whose needs change with advancing age. They are also designed with specific target dates to suit the individuals of different age groups considering their life expectancy.

A similar reasoning applies to the diversification of the asset category of bonds as well. Here one may buy different kinds of bonds, such as municipal and corporate and with different maturities. Again the alternative is to invest in a bond mutual fund which invests in municipal or corporate bonds of different investment grades and with different maturities.

With the above diversification in mind, the mutual fund companies offer mutual funds which invest in both stocks and bonds and these are known as the balanced funds.

11.9 Portfolio Rebalancing

It refers to bringing back the asset allocation to the original asset allocation mix. Rebalancing becomes necessary because over time the asset allocation mix is changed as some of the assets in the portfolio grow faster than others. For example, in normal market conditions the stocks are expected to grow faster than the bonds and the bonds faster than cash. In a market correction, it could be the other way round because the stocks go down faster while the bonds and cash might not be affected. The rebalancing may be done by selling parts of the appreciated assets and plowing the proceeds back into the other assets. This results in selling high and buying low which is the key to making profits. Alternatively, rebalancing may be done by adding fresh funds to the category of assets that have gone down in price. The problem with selling the assets in taxable accounts is that the capital gains taxes kick in along with the cost of trading which these days is fairly small. Rebalancing forces the investor to determine what to sell and when to sell it.

The next question is when the rebalancing of portfolio should be done. Some advocate that it should be done six monthly or once a year. Others recommend rebalancing when the relative weight of an asset class increases or decreases more than a certain percentage relative to the original allocation. Rebalancing is psychologically difficult because it involves selling appreciated assets and buying those that have not. The benefit of rebalancing is most evident during the periods of sharp market correction.

11.10 The Role of Robo Advisor in Asset Allocation

Robo advisors are a relatively new phenomenon. They have come into play because of the need to assist people with asset allocation and balancing while keeping costs low. Financial advice is a lucrative profession and is costly. The financial advisors charge a minimum of 1% fees on the account balances of half a million dollars or more. This amounts to a minimum of $5000 yearly and more on larger balances. The fees are larger on lower account balances and many advisors would not even be interested in such accounts. The reason of course is that the higher the account balance, the larger is the earning of the advisor. Whereas human financial advisors may advise on diverse financial matters, robo advisors assist normally with asset allocation and rebalancing only. Robo advisors use a human-created algorithm which is a complex mathematical formula that takes into account the investing goals, the timeline and the investment amount as input from the investor and the historical long-term performance data of the assets like stocks, bonds and cash instruments. The algorithm suggests an appropriate proportion of the assets. Robo advisors charge roughly 0.15 to 0.35% of the portfolio amount depending upon the size of the account. They rebalance the portfolio

periodically to keep it in harmony with the investor input. The major pitfall here is that in the case of market sell-off the investors have no human for advice and so could sell out of fear resulting in large losses.

Robo advisors are not suitable for complex situations involving the prioritization of goals such as saving for college education, paying down debt, saving for special needs etc., 401 Ks, pension or other employer-held savings plan, divorce etc. Some firms have started offering hybrid robo- advisory services where the services of a human advisor are added for an extra fees of about 0.25%. The examples of some of the firms offering such services are Charles Schwab, Fidelity, Bank of America, Morgan Stanley and Vanguard.

11.11 Summary

1. An asset class denotes a collection of the related securities which could be the stocks, bonds or cash equivalents. Here the stocks are one asset class, bonds another and cash investments the third asset class.
2. An asset class consists of many sub-asset classes. For example, stocks as an asset class might consist of many sub-asset classes

which could relate to different capitalizations, value or growth, and the origin in terms of the country or region. The same principle applies to other asset classes as well.

3. Asset allocation refers to the allocation of portfolio funds to different asset classes so as to obtain the maximum return with minimum risk in view of the return requirement, risk tolerance and the time horizon for investment.

4. One of the most important factors in asset allocation is the age of the person. The older the person is, the smaller should be the proportion of the riskier assets.

5. Asset allocation is considered to be a dynamic process which may involve different strategies. Some of these are the strategic asset allocation, constant-weighting allocation and tactical asset allocation.

6. Many model portfolios involving the three asset classes, namely equities, bonds and cash or cash equivalents have been suggested.

7. The asset allocation drifts with time and so requires portfolio rebalancing from time to time.

8. Robo advisors are getting fairly popular these days for portfolio allocation and rebalancing.

Suggested Action Items

Assemble the securities purchased as per suggested action in different chapters to give shape to your portfolio. Consider what other securities you would like to add to meet the requirement of diversification and rebalancing with regards to your age.

Chapter 12

Plan for Successful Investing

12.1 Introduction

The objective of this chapter is to prepare the investor for successful investing while stressing the principles covered in earlier chapters. It tells the investor to start with the development of an investment plan based on the current financial health, future needs, earning power and risk tolerance. It raises the awareness of tax implications and suggests how to reduce the effect of taxes by prudent investment decisions. It reviews the guidelines for buying and selling the stocks to maximize gains and reduce losses. It emphasizes that the bull and bear markets are an inevitable part of investing and so what to do in bear market crash.

12.2 Develop an Investment Plan and Philosophy

Investing is a rewarding but risky business. It is rewarding because it provides the pathway to building wealth. It is risky because one can lose a lot of money if not done properly. Recognize that the risk and reward are interrelated. This means that with higher risk comes a greater reward and vice versa. Therefore one needs to have a plan which is consistent with the goals and realistic in terms of the risks involved. Having a clear understanding of where you are and what you want to accomplish in the time horizon at your disposal is essential to develop a plan and the investment strategy to follow it. This gets complicated because the risk tolerance is difficult to assess as it depends not only on the emotional ability to withstand ups and downs in the portfolio but also on the current financial wellbeing.

Consider a young couple starting early in the career and interested in accumulating wealth over time to raise family and take care of the old age needs. The factor in favor of this couple is that it has a long time horizon. It can thus accept greater risk (volatility), as expected for the stocks, for the prospect of greater long-time return. On the other hand, a retired couple with limited means cannot afford to invest in risky investments because of the loss of the original investment and be left with no money to live on. These are the two extreme cases because some retirees with modest retirement savings could invest in both the fixed income investments and the dividend-paying blue chip stocks. Notice that the investment philosophy here is being governed by the risk and return considerations.

As discussed in the earlier chapter, the portfolio needs to be planned cognizant of the fact that the return is going to be based on the asset classes in the portfolio such as the equities, bonds and fixed income securities. As for the equities, their capitalization and growth versus value characteristics are important. As for the bonds, their ratings in terms of the quality and duration are important. Thus there are many factors to consider and could be quite confusing if tackled together. In order to make the process simple, we will follow here the approach in steps and bring in the related factors as and when necessary.

12.3 Developing the Portfolio

Here we start with an outline of the portfolio and fill in the details later. This outline will depend upon the investor's situation. For example, for a young couple early in the career there is need to set aside some money for savings. How much that depends upon the individual situation. In most countries where people are savings minded, people save at least 10% of their income. It is recognized that it is not always easy, so save whatever you can. It is essential for a secure future. It does take a sacrifice to build financial security and is as important as food and medicine. Since this is the beginning, it is suggested to invest this money in an index fund, preferably SPY, because this will provide diversification in itself. Remember that SPY is a collection of 500 large cap stocks representing the companies from different segments. It is possible to buy any number of the shares of SPY. Once you have these shares, monitor them from time to time because it will give you the feel how stock prices vary on day-to-day basis. In other words, it will prepare you psychologically to the fluctuations in stock price and you will stop panicking after some time with every price drop.

The prudent strategy is to buy more shares when the price drops. We call it buying low. If it is not possible, make it a habit to invest at least the same amount of money every month (or every alternate month) irrespective of the stock price. This is called compounding and in no time you will be building wealth. Some people might prefer to do this compounding exercise using a large cap stock mutual fund or a balance fund (which is the hybrid of stocks and bonds), through regular payroll deduction which the fund company will do on your behalf.

It is recognized here that everyone's situation is different. If you need urgently to save some money for tuition or down payment on car or house, you could do the same thing by buying the certificates of deposit. Remember that the return from the stock market has the potential to be the highest but not guaranteed because it may also result in losses in the short term. If past market performance is any guide, stock market is one of the most promising approach to building wealth over an extended period of time. Remember that time is a very important factor in this approach and so the earlier you start, the greater are the chances of success.

Once you get used to the stock market behavior, you may add other stocks gradually paying attention to building a diversified portfolio by adding stocks of the companies in different businesses and capitalizations, both domestic and international, and an assortment of bonds with different maturities.

As emphasized in Chapter 11, the asset allocation depends upon the age of the person. Thus a person in the middle of career would be better off starting with a hybrid of stocks and bonds, selected individually or using mutual funds and ETFs. Similarly a person close to or in retirement would tilt towards the bonds and/or stocks with good dividends. If this person has enough wealth and is not dependent for living upon the income generated from investments, he/she can invest heavily in stocks for greater return potential.

Once we know what we want to accomplish in terms of the portfolio, we need to fund it in order to give it a shape. This will require the understanding developed in earlier chapters in the book with regards to the basics of buying and selling of stocks, bonds, ETFs and mutual funds. We discuss below some other aspects which deserve consideration for successful investing.

12.4 Tax Considerations in developing the Portfolio

Any transaction involving money raises the possibility of taxation. Since stock market investing has to do with money changing hands, it is subject to taxation unless done in a tax-exempt account. This requires that the portfolio is constructed in a way that it produces maximum tax efficiency.

The investments in IRA, Roth IRA and 401(k) or 403(b) accounts are tax- free. This means that with the stocks or mutual funds bought in these accounts, the dividends and capital gains are not subject to taxes. With the exception of Roth IRA, these accounts are taxed at ordinary rates when mandatory withdrawals required by law at later age are taken. Most municipal bonds are exempt from federal taxes and some also from state taxes in the state where issued. 529 College Savings Accounts allow people to save after-tax money and get tax-deferred growth along with federal income tax-free withdrawals when used for qualified expenses.

As for the investment in stocks, bonds and mutual funds in normal accounts, the dividends and capital gains are taxed at rates which are different for different income levels. There is no tax on the dividends and capital gains for people in the lowest two income tax brackets of 10% and 15%. The maximum income corresponding to these brackets in the year 2017 is $37,950 for singles and $75,900 for married couples filing jointly. The people in higher tax brackets are taxed on their investment income at 15-20 % rate when qualified (holding period of one year or more) and at the effective tax rate of the tax-payer when non-qualified (holding period of less than one year). When the stock, bond, mutual fund or ETF is sold, it is subject to capital gains or losses: short term if held for less than one year or long term if held for more than one year. The short term loss is disallowed if the same or an identical security is bought within 30 days of the prior sale of the security. Then the short term gains are offset by the short term losses and the long term gains by the long term losses. If there is a net capital loss, the maximum loss allowed against the taxable income is $3,000 for a married couple filing jointly and the excess is carried over to the following years.

The corresponding deduction for single filing status is $1,500. The tax rates described here are mentioned only for guidance. They are too complicated to describe and further they may change anytime. It is therefore advised to check for the current rates.

While trying to multiply wealth by investing, equally important is how much you get to keep after taxation. The following strategies are used to manage taxes:

1. Defer taxes by investing in IRAs, 401(k) or 403(b) accounts. Roth IRAs are great back-up saving accounts for those starting out because they could access their contributions tax-free if they ever needed to. Those in high income brackets, not allowed Roth IRA, should contribute to traditional IRA and take the tax deduction.

2. Invest in federal income tax free municipal bonds with state tax exemption if possible. The higher your tax bracket, the more benefit you get from this tax-exemption.

3. Keep taxes low by meeting the requirement of long-term capital gains and qualified dividends. Aim for the short term losses.

4. Avoid frequent trading because it triggers the prospect of taxation.

5. Invest in mutual funds with low distributions and low turnover rates.

6. Put the investments that generate large taxable income in accounts that are tax-sheltered.

7. Avoid purchasing mutual fund shares just before the distribution date because as a shareholder you become liable for income tax on the distribution.

8. Manage your taxes by tax-loss harvesting. The latter refers to selling the investments in which you have losses. By selling such investments, you have the loss that may be utilized to offset gains elsewhere.

9. If considering charitable donations, consider donating securities with large capital appreciation. By doing this, you avoid paying taxes on the capital appreciation while getting a large charitable deduction from your taxable income.

10. If subject to mandatory withdrawal from your IRA account, donate money from this account directly to the charitable organization. This will meet your withdrawal requirement while exempting you from taxation on this money.

Finally while tax consideration are important for building wealth, the investing strategy is even more important. The potential benefits of any strategy need to be considered in the context of the overall investing plan.

Table 12.1 provides the recommended matching of the different types of investments with taxable, tax-deferred and tax-exempt accounts.

Table 12.1 Matching of investments with different types of accounts.

Investment description	Taxable account	Tax-deferred account	Tax-exempt account
Tax-free municipal bonds and municipal mutual funds	yes		
Equity securities held long term	yes		
Equity index funds held long term	yes		
Tax-managed mutual funds and accounts	yes		
High turnover stock mutual funds		yes	yes
Taxable bond and bond mutual funds		yes	yes

12.5 Essentials of Successful Investing

The success with investing is going to involve the following three things: setting up the goals realistically, buying the right kind of securities, and selling these securities for maximum gains while minimizing losses. We examine them below:

(a) Setting the right goals and expectations

1. Set up your investment goals based on the assessment of your situation. These should take into account your needs, objectives, age, risk tolerance and ambition in life. The goals should be

realistic in view of your abilities and the earnings prospects.

2. Work out a strategy to meet your goals. Keep your expectations within reason.

3. Consider all the investment possibilities and develop over time a portfolio consisting of fixed income investments, bonds and stocks. Diversify in each category to reduce risk. Add some real estate either through real estate investment trust or rental property.

4. Understand how each asset class is affected by the economic, political and other conditions. If interest rates are stable and likely to remain so, bonds can provide a good return. They are excellent bets if the interest rates are falling. Avoid bonds if interest rates are rising or appear to rise. Stocks do well when interest rates are low because they have less competition from fixed income investments. They do well also in low inflation environment or when the economic activity picks up due to better earnings prospects.

5. Adjust the asset allocation at least once a year.

(b) Buying the right securities at the right time

1. When investing in the stock market, consider that you are buying a piece of business and not the stock. If you do not understand the business, don't buy it. Look for the quality businesses with moat. Never invest in speculative companies particularly those that trade over the counter.

2. Invest in the stocks of established companies, preferably in timely industries, paying attention to the economy such as the interest rate, employment, inflation/deflation, etc.

3. Look for the investor-friendly companies which have the interest of the shareholders. Such companies have stock purchase plans to benefit the shareholders and have the track record of rational allocation of capital.

4. While looking for buying the stock, watch for the stock with rising volume and with rising prices. This indicates more buyers than sellers and is positive for the stock price.

5. Don't dwell on the price of stock. Instead study the underlying

business, its earnings potential, future prospects and so on.

6. Take time for the stock price to get depressed so as to make buying possible with a margin of safety. Pounce when the three variables come together: a strong business with an enduring competitive advantage, strong management, and low stock price

7. Learn to like a sinking market because it presents buying opportunity. If the herd starts running away from a good stock, get ready to run toward it. The legendary investor Warren Buffet said "Be fearful when others are greedy and greedy when others are fearful. Buy when people are selling and sell when people are buying. Be ready when the opportunity strikes."

8. Buy great businesses and hold them for years. Frequent trading is the hallmark of overactive investors who tend to wind up with more losses than gains.

9. In a rising market, buy the stock when it is on the upside move.

10. Never risk more than 10% of your capital on any single purchase. Instead try to have a portfolio of companies from different sectors.

11. When making a large purchase, consider spacing your purchases over a period of time. In volatile markets, use the dollar cost averaging technique.

12. Do not get overly concerned about the temporary price swings in stocks or the market. Quality and value will be profitable if patient.

13. Do not get caught up with the masses and hit the panic button when markets fall.

14. Do not buy mutual fund shares close to year end before distributions. The reason for this is that as the owner of the mutual fund you become liable to pay taxes on the distributions.

(c) Selling the securities at the right time

1. For a stock just bought or appreciated less than 10%, sell if the stock drops 10% from its highest price reached.

2. Sell if the company reduces sales or earnings forecast or announces the cut in dividend.

3. Sell if the company is losing market share.

4. Watch out if the company restates financials. This happens mostly from overstating sales or understating costs to hype the reported earnings. It may be wise to sell at this time.
5. Sell if the prospects of the company deteriorate as in housing because of the rise in interest rates.
6. The drop in the same store or restaurant sales calls for caution and the sale of the stock should be considered as an option.
7. Watch for the decline in operating margin. Declining operating margins signal deteriorating market share, reduced profits or both. Small variations in the operating margin are normal but a drop of 15% or greater year over year calls for action.
8. If the valuation of the stock is much higher than the fair market value, consider selling at least some shares.
9. Very few stocks continue to trade far above the average PE ratio of their industry or their own average PE of the last five years. In such cases, it is better to sell a little early than to take the risk of overstaying the market.
10. Watch with caution if the price of stock drops below its 50-day moving average line. A steep drop from there in the price of stock approaching or crossing the 200-day moving average line calls for the sale of the stock. If not already sold, the stock should definitely be sold if it has crossed the 200-day moving average line.
11. If the company is in an announced or rumored takeover, consider selling for a known profit rather than holding out for the last conceivable dollar.
12. Aim for the short-terms losses and the long-term gains to get the benefit in taxes. The investments held for more than one year qualify for the long term gain or loss and those held for less than one year for the short term gain or loss.

12.6 Evaluating Market Levels

The stock market never goes straight up or down and again with no regularity. It often does so in bits and pieces. When the market is elevated, we call it the bull market and when it is depressed, it is known as the bear market. No one knows if the market is going up or down next and so it is just a guessing game. The bull market is the dream of every investor but it is not always the reality. The investor would of course like to know the direction of the market so that he or she could get out in time if it was going to drop big. In this context, it should be kept in mind that the market rarely stays at extremes. It eventually moves back to a normal level which could be different every time. It does so sometimes fast but at other times it may take long. Not only that but also the peaks and bottoms in any cycle are known only after the fact. It is thus a guessing game at best.

The following is the history of bear and bull markets [From DrDoolittle, May 5, 2013, http://www.gold-eagle.com/article/history-us-bear-bull-markets- 1929]:

(a) Bear Market

There have been 25 Bear Markets since 1929 with the average frequency of 3.4 years. The average bear market period lasted 10 months and the average bear market loss was -35%. The smallest loss was -21% in the year 1949 and the largest loss was -62% in the year 1932. The last bear market ended in March 2009.

(b) Bull
Market

There have been 25 Bull Markets since 1929. The average bull market period lasted 31 months. The average bull market gain was +104%. The smallest gain was +21% in 2001, and the largest gain was +582% in the period 1987- 2000.

From the above, it is clear that the bear and bull markets occur at random. Their magnitude and frequency is irregular. There is no way to predict them. The present bull market is unusually long 10 years old compared to the average frequency of 3.4 years.

The two measures often cited with respect to the bull or bear market are the dividend yield and the P/E ratio of the broad market index S&P 500 with the ticker symbol SPY. Since the earning does not change on a daily basis, this means that the P/E of SPY will be elevated in a bull market. As for the dividend yield (defined as the ratio of dividend to the price of SPY), it will be low because of the high value of SPY with the dividend value unchanged.

The reverse of this will be the case in a bear market. In view of these observations, these two ratios are commonly cited in support of the impending bull and bear markets.

Table 12.2 gives the range of P/E and dividend yield values for SPY in the decades shown. It should be noted that both the P/E and the dividend yield have wide ranges. Furthermore the highest P/E and the lowest dividend yield do not correspond to each other in terms of the time. Thus these two ratios are not good forecasters of the bull and bear markets. In spite of this, because of their simplicity, they are often quoted as the indicators of the bull and bear

markets. It will, however, be reasonable to say that if P/E is too high, the market is vulnerable and can crash on any bad development. How high no one knows. Roughly speaking, the SPY P/E of above 17-18 should call for caution in this regard.

Table 12.2 Historical S&P 500 P/E and Dividend Yield ranges for the decades shown.

Decades	P/E range	Dividend Yield range
1960s	13 – 23.8	2.8-3.9
1970s	7.2-20.1	2.7-5.9
9180s	6.9-22.7	2.7-6.4
1990s	13.4-35.4	1.2-4.0
2000s	15.7-29.3	1.1-1.9

12.7 Factors to consider for Market Correction

Since market corrections have severe consequences, the investor needs to be on the alert. The following are some of the items deserving attention of the investor with regards to market correction:

1. Is the market overpriced in terms of the valuation?
2. Are certain sectors overheated? Are the prices of the stocks in that sector not supported by the underlying fundamentals?

3. Is the economy heading toward recession?
4. Is the Federal Reserve monetary policy tightening?
5. Is there a spike occurring in commodity prices?
6. Is the economy of our trading partners such as Europe, UK, China etc. getting worse and likely to affect our trade?

If the answer to anyone of the above questions is in the affirmative, there are grounds to become cautious. This is supported by Table 12.3 which covers a period of about half a century. The bear market crash of 1970 occurred because of the civil unrest connected with black uprising, high inflation and aggressive fed tightening. It lasted for 18 months and the market correction was 36%. In 1973 the crisis was precipitated by the OPEC oil embargo so that the gas prices went sky high. This brought recession and the market correction was about 48%. The market correction of 1980 was caused by the recession resulting from very high interest rates and aggressive fed tightening. The correction here was 27%. The next market correction in 1987 occurred because of the overheating of markets from program trading, and the next two in the years 2000 and 2007 from extreme valuations arising from dotcom bubble, financial crisis and the resulting recession. These two corrections were 49% and 57% respectively. *So any time there is market exuberance, extreme price hike, aggressive fed tightening or the likelihood of recession, there is a probability of market crash.* Note further that these corrections are severe approaching 50% in some cases and they may last for about one to three years.

Table 12.3 Data of the bear markets of the past half century. Source: FactSet, NBER, Robert Schiller, Standard &Poor's, J P Morgan.

Market correction	Market peak	Bear Return	Duration, months	Environment
Tech Crash of 1970 – Economic overheating, Civil unrest	Nov 1968	-36%	18	Recession, Commodity spike, Aggressive Fed
Stagflation – OPEC oil embargo	Jan 1973	-48%	21	Recession, Commodity Spike
Volker tightening - Whip inflation now	Nov 1980	-27%		Recession, Commodity spike, Aggressive Fed
1987 – Program trading, overheating markets	Aug 1987	-34%	3	
Tech bubble – Extreme valuations, .com boom/bust	May 2000	-49%	31	Recession
Global Financial Crisis – Leverage housing, Lehman collapse	Oct. 2007	-57%	17	Recession, Aggressive Fed, Commodity spike

12.8 Strategies for Bear Market Crash

From the above discussion, we have seen that market crashes are inevitable and they occur due to the excesses in the market. There is no recurrence regularity and they occur unpredictably. As such there is no foolproof way to predict and save your portfolio from the losses when the crash occurs. Getting out of the market in anticipation of the crash is not foolhardy because of the loss of appreciation while waiting for the correction to develop. The best an investor can do is to take prudent steps to minimize the losses. These are described below:

1. When you invest in the market, you do not need to be "all in" or "all out". The prudent investors always keep some cash handy to put in the market in case the market goes down. This is the cash ready to invest at the lower prices in the event of a severe market correction. Think of selling some stocks to raise cash when the market is high. How much is a matter of personal judgment but

   20 to 30 percent of the portfolio is considered reasonable. Lightening the portfolio is advisable anyway in keeping with the principle "buy low and sell high". It will also increase the liquidity avoiding the need to sell in panic if the correction is protracted.

2. Check if the portfolio is diversified and balanced. The diversification into different assets is needed so that the portfolio is not badly hurt if any particular asset class takes a hard beating. Rebalancing is needed because over time the portfolio could have gotten concentrated in one kind of assets such as stocks. If so, increase the investment in bonds and cash.

3. Get rid of the high-flyer stocks with lofty valuations based on earnings, sales and asset values. These are the kinds of companies that decline most in market corrections. Instead reinvest in stocks of moderate valuations, low beta and stable blue chip companies preferably with dividends. Alternatively invest in an ETF or a diversified domestic stock mutual fund which pays dividends, such as Vanguard Dividend Growth fund (VDIGX).

4. Place a trailing stop particularly on those stocks that have appreciated considerably. Such stocks normally undergo severe corrections in the event of a market crash. A trailing stop generates an automatic sell order as soon as the stock hits the stop order set on its way down. How much below the highest price reached by the stock should the trailing stop be set is the investor's choice. It is normally 15 to 20%, with more volatile stocks needing a higher percentage. The disadvantage of a stop order is that sometimes the market goes down just enough to trigger the stop order while snapping back again thus depriving the investor from the bounce in stock price.

5. Another alternative is to buy the inverse ETF which goes in the inverse direction to that of the underlying market. This means that if the market goes down, the inverse ETF goes up. Thus the increase in the price of the ETF partially compensates for the loss in the value of the portfolio. Note that the inverse ETF acts like an insurance where you pay for its purchase but benefit only when the ETF goes down. Inverse ETFs are available for many broad market and sector indexes.

6. People adept in options buy put options. A put option is the
   option purchased by the owner of stock that allows him/her to sell the
   stock at a predetermined price (known as the strike price) even
   when the stock is trading at a lower price. There is an expiration
   date for the option after which the option becomes worthless. The
   option is exercised only if the stock price goes below the strike price
   while it is active. So the option may or may not be exercised but it
   costs money to the buyer anyway. *The options are not
   recommended for the readers of this book because they are risky
   and require understanding and mastery of the practice.*

12.9 The Argument for Buy and Hold Investing

The biggest nightmare of an investor is to be wiped out during a bear market crash. In view of this, it is smart to use at least some of the strategies described in the previous section. In any case, the investor would be better off having exercised due diligence with respect to the items 1 to 3 because portfolio diversification and rebalancing are essential irrespective of the direction of the market. The second requirement is that the investor has some cash ready to invest in case the market drops suddenly. This enables the investor to invest at rock bottom prices thereby recouping some of the losses. Given enough time the investor may even come out ahead with the recovery in the market.

As for the trailing stop, they often put the investor out of the stock at the wrong time. It has been found that sometimes the stock dives momentarily on some kind of bad news thereby activating the trailing stop but recovering soon after it was activated. So exercise of the stop order is not necessarily the right move all the time. *The inverse ETF and the put options are risky maneuvers and are not recommended for our readers.*

The question then is what the sudden market crash will do to our portfolio. It will certainly precipitate losses but more often than not these losses are short- lived. This is so because the market often tends to recover fast at least partially. Given enough time, the market may recover fully. This assertion is based on the historical record of the market. In the stock market patience is virtue and the market has always gone up over a period of time. For example, the Dow climbed from 2,002 to 20,268 over a period of January 1987 to January 2017. This is about ten times over a period of 30 years. During this period, the doomed Black Monday Crash of 22.6% occurred in October 1987 and the financial crisis precipitated in September 2008 because of the

bankruptcy filing of Lehman Brothers. Dow dived to 6,547 in September 2008 but recovered to 10,000 in October 2009. These observations of the past history of the market lead us to the following conclusions:

1. The market goes up and down on a daily basis but it always goes up over time. The latter is because the market behavior is affected by the prosperity of the businesses which in a thriving national economy have nowhere to go but up.

2. While the correction in market may be large but the recovery may also be rapid. Thus if you get out of the market because of the market crash, you will be deprived of the rapid recovery which may occur following it.

3. Going back to the past century, it is seen that stocks have produced an average return of 8-10% per year. In some years, they have lost but in others they have gained more than that. Thus stock market investing is for the long haul.

4. Do not attempt market timing because that is a sure recipe for disaster. There is no way to predict highs and lows in the market except to find out after the fact. No one even the market 'Gurus' have the ability to do that and so shy away from this practice.

12.10 Summary

1. The investor should start by developing an investment plan based on the needs and the time horizon. The plan should be realistic in view of the funding ability and the risk level appropriate for the age of the investor.

2. The effort should be made to invest in the companies with economic moat at discount. The investments should be allowed to compound over time.

3. Follow the guidelines as stated for buying and selling the stocks and invest only in the companies with economic moat.

4. Be aware of the economic conditions and factor them in your investment decisions.

5. Investing comes with the tax consequences. The tax awareness can be used to match investments with the proper type of accounts to reduce tax liability. Furthermore the tax burden can be reduced by timing the purchase and sale of the investments.

6. The past history of the market reveals that ups and down in the stock market are normal and cannot be avoided.

7. The bear markets are devastating. Some of the measures to reduce the onslaught of the bear market have been suggested.

8. There is no sure way to predict the tops and bottoms in the market. These are determined only after the fact. In the case of market crash, the investor needs to exercise patience by staying put because over time the markets recover.

Chapter 13

Financial Resources

13.1 Introduction

There are a large number of resources available for broadening the financial understanding. Some of these are in the form of magazines and newspapers which cover the broad topics including the interest rates, bank accounts, credit cards and the economy in general. Some of them provide specific recommendations related to the buying and selling of bonds, stocks and mutual funds. The media and the internet sites also help in expanding the financial literacy. There are publications which discuss and recommend the specific stocks, bonds and mutual funds for investment and even provide model portfolios. In addition to these, there are websites which provide current financial data while the market is open. The objective of this chapter is to introduce some of these resources to the reader.

13.2 Importance of Financial Resources

With respect to investing, there is a lot of help available from the financial media and the publications. These resources provide information relevant to all kinds of financial topics and in particular to investing in the stocks, bonds, mutual funds and ETFS. We have already looked at the Yahoo Finance (http://finance.yahoo.com/) and Morningstar (www.morningstar .com /) websites. Some of the other websites which cover the business news are www.cnbc.com, www.money.cnn.com, www.investors.com, www.bloomberg.com, www.marketwatch.com and www.zacks.com. Then there are publications available on subscription basis such as the investment advisory reports, financial magazines, newspapers, etc. The list is large and so we will be covering only some of the publications that are particularly useful in the selection of investments. While some publications follow up on their recommendations, many others do not. There is always an inclination on the part of the investor to make an investment based on the recommendation in a television program or in one of the publications. Such a recommendation should be treated as a lead idea but further evaluation is strongly recommended before investment. It is so because the revenue and the earnings forecast, financial health, market demand of the products, etc. may change along with the economy and the health of the related industry in the current environment. It should be realized that these events change and the smart investors stay ahead of such developments.

13.3 Value Line Investment Survey

It is one of the highly regarded and widely used independent investment publication. It has its own website www.valueline.com which provides information about the publication and the subscription price. It is somewhat expensive for individual subscription. It is generally available free for consultation in most public libraries. If you have access to it, it is recommended that you consult it on a regular basis.

The Value Line Publication comes in two editions:

(1) Standard Edition

(2) Small and Mid-Cap Edition

The Standard Edition covers large and medium cap stocks and tracks approximately 1800 stocks in over 90 industries. The Small and Mid-Cap Edition also tracks 1800 companies but in the small cap category. The coverage is in three parts: 1. Summary and Index, 2. Selection and Opinion, and 3. Ratings and Reports. These are described below.

 1. Summary and Index

This part summarizes the financial information relevant to investing for the companies that it covers. It also serves as the index for the companies discussed in the part entitled Ratings and Reports. The following is the information presented in tabular form in the Summary and Index:

- Page No. in Ratings and Reports ·
Stock name and ticker symbol
- Price of stock
- Timeliness, Safety and Technical Ratings on the scale of 1 to 5, 1 being the highest and 5 the lowest
- β for the stock
- 3-5 year appreciation estimate ·
Price to earnings ratio (P/E)
- Estimated yield next 12 months ·
Estimated earnings to year end ·
Industry rank
- Latest earnings per share (E/sh)
- Dividends for the quarter ended and the year ago

In addition to the above, the Summary and Index has tables with the following information:

- Industries in order of timeliness
- Stocks moving up and down in timeliness rank ·
Timely stocks in timely industries
- Stocks ranked 1 and 2 for timeliness and for relative safety ·
Stocks with the highest dividends
- Stocks with the highest 3-5 year appreciation potential ·
Stocks ranked for the highest cash flow
- The best and worst performing stocks
- Stocks with the widest discount from book value ·
Stocks with the lowest and the highest P/E, etc.

2. Selection and Opinion

In this part of the Value Line Investment Survey, the following information is presented:

- Economic and stock market commentary
- Portfolios of stocks with the following criteria:

(a) above average price potential

(b) income and price appreciation potential

(c) long term growth potential

(d) above average dividend yields

(e) high dividend growth with low risk **(f)** growth stocks with low risk

(g) timely stocks with high price and earnings momentum

· Industry analysis
· Plots tracking the economy ·
Major insider transactions
· 7 best and 7 worst performing industries in the last six months ·
Data on economy, market averages, etc.

3. Ratings and Reports

This part of the Value Line Investment Survey provides detailed coverage of the companies in such a way that all 1700 companies are covered once in 13 weeks (that is every quarter). It provides an overview of the related industry which is followed by the coverage on specific companies in that particular industry. The noteworthy feature here is that the information on each company is presented in an identical format and is limited to one page. The reports are thus easy to follow and the reader knows a priori what type of information is available in them. The format of the report is presented in the next section.

13.4 Value Line Ratings and Report Format

The main features of this report are described below:

1. The top line gives the factual information for the company. It gives the recent stock price, P/E ratio, relative P/E ratio, and dividend yield. Here relative P/E is the stock's current P/E divided by the median P/E for all the stocks under the Value Line review.

2. Below this is provided the Value Line's assessment of the

company in terms of the timeliness, safety, and technical position. This assessment is on the scale of 1 to 5 where 1 is the highest and 5 the lowest. Below this is the Value Line's projection for the price of stock 3-5 years later, both on the high and low ends. Further below is the information on the insider decisions to buy and sell options, and the institutional buy and sell decisions and the holdings of the stock.

3. It shows the stock price plot over a period of ten years. Below this is the exhaustive data relevant to the stock for 10-15 years presented in a tabular form. Some of the data items are revenues, cash flow, earnings, dividends, capital spending, book value, operating margin, net profit margin, return on total capital and shareholder equity etc.

4. It gives the data on the financial condition of the company in terms of the current assets and current liabilities.

5. It shows the breakup of the revenues and earnings per share for the last five years.

6. Lastly it provides the assessment of the company reflecting on the past problems, future hurdles and the outlook. It provides justification for the assessment provided in item 2 above.

It should be noted from the above description that the Value Line Report condenses a lot of pertinent information about the company along with its evaluation on one page. It also makes convenient for the investor to do his/her own analysis based on the past earnings, PE ratios, revenues, cash flow, profit margin, return on investment, book value, etc. The unique feature of Value Line Report is that it provides the information for all the companies in the same format and is limited to one page. This makes it easy for the reader to follow and analyze.

In the year 2017, Value Line started a new service "Value Line Select: ETFs". Each month it selects one ETF that offers the best risk/reward ratio and hence expected to outperform the market. Each monthly report includes the state of the economy, overview of the industry pertinent to the selected ETF, and the supporting tables and charts for the selected ETF.

13.5 Standard and Poor's (S&P Capital IQ) Report

Standard and Poor's (S&P) is an investment advisory service. It publishes individual reports on the specific stocks. This report is generally available on the brokers' websites free of charge. It gives the last stock price and the 12- month target price of the stock along with star ranking. S&P rates stocks on the scale of 1 to 5 stars (*) with 1 being the least desirable and 5 the most desirable. Thus 5* is Strong Buy and 4* is Buy. 3* refers to Hold recommendation. Below this section is the information on the sector and the sub-industry to which this company belongs. In the next section below it, the important statistics for the company are given. These include the trailing 12- month EPS along with the S&P operating EPS estimates for the next year and

the following year. Next it gives the trailing 12-month PE and the PE based on the current year's earnings. In addition to the above, it gives the 52-week stock price range, market capitalization, beta, yield, institutional ownership and S&P Credit Rating.

The graphical section gives the stock price variation, the volume of stock traded, 10-week and 30-week moving average lines, relative strength plot etc. for the last five years.

On the right side, the Analyst's Risk Assessment is provided. Below this is presented the quarterly data for Revenues and Earnings per share for the last five years, including the dividend information.

On the bottom left side in the highlights section, a brief description of the sales and growth expectation of the company products is given. On the right side of this, the Investment Rationale/ Risk for the company is provided. It includes comments on the suitability of the company for investment in terms of its products and earnings. It is followed by the discussion related to the evaluation of stock, risk factor and the target price calculation.

For the companies that S&P does not provide star ranking, it provides information in a concise format.

13.6 The Outlook

It is a publication of the Standard and Poor's targeted for individual investors. It uses the same star ranking system as discussed in the previous section. The weekly issues of the Outlook include different kinds of model portfolios some of which are listed below:

(a) High Quality Capital Appreciation Portfolio – It includes the stocks that have 4-star or 5-star ranking in addition to the Quality ranking of A- or better. The quality ranking is based on 10 years of above average earnings and dividend growth.

(b) Platinum Portfolio – It includes the stocks with star ranking of 5 and also the fair value ranking of 5. The fair value ranking refers to the stocks significantly undervalued relative to S&P 500.

(c) Small and Mid-cap Growth portfolio

(d) Top Ten Model portfolio – It is designed with the objective of high potential for capital appreciation over the next 12 months.

(e) Total Return Model portfolio – The focus in this portfolio is on maximizing the long term total return.

(f) Industry Momentum Model portfolio – Here the top stocks from the industries represented in S&P 500 are included based on their relative strength.

The weekly issues discuss also the specific stocks, focus stocks, groups of stocks, and fixed income and exchange-traded funds (ETFs). In addition to these, the financial topics such as the economic prospects, technical analysis, foreign markets and financial planning strategies are also covered.

13.7 Barron's and the Wall Street Journal

Both of these publications are from the Dow Jones and Company. The Wall Street Journal is a reputable daily financial newspaper. Apart from the current news items, it includes the news related to the financial topics such as the interest rate, credit, economy, jobs, legislation, employment, taxes, etc. It also talks about the specific companies affected by a new legislation, recall, technical or material development.

Barron's is a weekly publication available both in print and online. It is a popular publication sought after by the serious investors. It provides a wealth of information related to investing along with the recommendation on different kinds of investments. Barron's is comprised of two parts. The first part discusses the events in the past week under the general heading Up & Down Wall Street. It then includes the articles related to investing and also provides the recommendations on specific investments. The second part is the 'Market Week' which under the heading 'The Trader' discusses the market changes in the last week at home and abroad. It gives the plots of the Dow Jones Industrials, S&P 500, Nasdaq Composite and Barron's 400 for the past 52 weeks. It covers the important events affecting the stock prices of some companies. Apart from the US market, it includes the coverage of the markets in Asia, Europe and the emerging nations. There is a sampling of the Research Reports and the investment recommendations on specific companies. The rest of the section provides market statistics along with the prices of common and preferred stocks, bonds, ETFs and mutual funds. Included with this are also sometimes the special reports such as the Best of Breed Wealth Managers, Ranking of Hedge Funds, Advice for Families with Assets of $5 Million or More, Quarterly Performance of Mutual Funds, and Quarterly Round Table Discussion in which the panelists discuss the economic and stock market views and make recommendations on the specific investments.

13.8 Investor's Business Daily

It is the newspaper targeted specifically to the individual investors. It covers the national and international financial news and provides detailed information about the stocks, mutual funds, commodities, and other financial products. Some of the important features of the newspaper include market updates and stock analysis, daily and weekly price and volume charts, list of the stocks on the move and their expanded discussion, stock screens, industry group leaders, etc.

The newspaper is known for its unique stock tables which include the following five SmartSelect measurements:

> 1. Earnings per share rank for the past five years

2. Relative price strength rank for the past 12 months
3. Industry group relative strength
4. Overall evaluation of sales, profit margin and return on equity
5. Accumulation (stock being bought) vs. distribution (stock being sold) for the past three months.

These five measurements along with the weighting given to the earnings per share and the relative price strength are used to arrive at a SmartSelect composite rating. The rating is on a scale of 1 to 99 with 99 being the best.

13.9 Internet Resources

(a) CNNMoney (http://money.cnn.com)

It is purely a financial site with subheadings such as the business, markets, investing, economy, personal finance, etc. In the Business section, it provides current news on the specific businesses. In the Market section, it provides the stock market overview including the Gainers and Losers in the US Stock Market, World Stock Market Indices, leading world currencies relative to the US dollar, commodity price changes, Treasury bond yields, and the prices of some mutual funds and exchange traded funds (ETFs). This broad market category has many sub categories which are listed below:

Premarket - refers to premarket trading.

After-hours - refers to aftermarket trading.

Stocks - stock price changes for the big gainers and losers.

Market movers - stocks with big changes in price up and down.

Dow 30 - price changes for the stocks in the Dow Jones Industrial index.

Bonds – US Treasury bond yields and the yields of investment grade and high yield corporate bonds.

Currencies – US dollar equivalence of major world currencies.

Mutual funds – NAV (net asset values) of the biggest mutual funds and those in the biggest gainers and losers category over one month to a year period.

ETFs – top and bottom ETFs.

World Markets – major world stock market indices and the companies in the biggest gainer and loser categories.

(b) Business Week (www.businessweek.com)

This internet site provides the business news in general.

(c) CNBC TV Channel and Website

It is an American basic cable and satellite business news television channel that is owned by the NBC Universal News Group. It covers the business headlines and provides the live coverage of financial markets. It is a very popular channel watched by the millions of people interested in the stock market.

Similar information is also available on the internet site www.cnbc.com.

Morningstar (http://www.morningstar.com/)

It is a very informative site which gives financial data on the stocks, bonds, ETFs and mutual funds. The data is useful in the analysis of these investments. The site is famous for the star ranking of mutual funds and ETFs. It is a very popular site used by the individual investors for the selection of investments.

Yahoo Finance (https://finance.yahoo.com/)

It is one of the most useful sites which provides all kinds of financial data. We have referred to this site exclusively in this book.

13.10 Magazines

Kiplinger's Personal Finance - Advice on investments, financial decisions, issues related to general finances

Forbes – updated news pertaining to business and finance

Fortune – famous for coverage of topmost Fortune 500 companies

Bloomberg Businessweek – financial news, stock advice, in-depth coverage on major businesses

13.11 Investment Advisory Services

These provide specific recommendations on the investments. They are too many to list and so only some of these are listed below:

Common Sense Investment Newsletter

Dow Theory Forecasts
Forbes Growth Investor

Inves Tech Market Analyst

Inves Tech Mutual Fund Advisor
Kiplinger's Investing for Income
Louis Navellier's Blue Chip Growth Letter
Morningstar Stock Investor

Motley Fool Stock Advisor The
Blue Chip Investor
Zack's Advisor

13.12 Summary

1. The financial publications have a lot of educational value. They provide timely information on the items related to economy, business and investments.

2. The Value Line Investment Survey is one of the most important publications for a serious investor. It consists of three parts: Summary and Index, Selection and Opinion, and Ratings and Reports. In the Summary and Index part, the basic information is condensed in a few pages on the companies that it covers. The Ratings and Reports part of the Value Line Investment Survey provides detailed coverage of the companies on a weekly basis in such a way that all 1700 companies are covered once in 13 weeks (that is every quarter).

3. Standard and Poor's Reports are very helpful in making investment decisions. They provide one-page summary of the financial aspects of the company along with the star rating and the target price of the stock.

4. The Outlook publication provides recommendations on the different kinds of stock portfolios and the discussion on topics useful for the investors.

5. Barron's is a weekly publication which provides the discussion of the markets in the past week and the comments on stocks from the investment perspective. This is a very useful publication for serious investors.

6. Kiplinger's Personal Finance and Fortune are the financial magazines which cover general business and financial topics of interest. They provide limited recommendations on the stocks, mutual funds and ETFs as well.

Chapter 14

Economic Factors in Investment Decisions

14.1 Introduction

In this chapter, the relevant measures of economy and the effect of fiscal and monetary policies on the economy are covered. Since investing has to do with money, it is directly or indirectly related to the prevailing economic conditions. An understanding of the economic factors is therefore desirable for prudent investment decisions. The business news both in print and media refers to many economic measures that describe the status of the national economy as well as the fiscal and monetary policies to correct or improve the economic condition of the nation. It is therefore necessary to be familiar with the economic parameters. The ability to gage the status of the economy and the expected result from the corrective measures adopted by the government is also important for prudent investing.

14.2 Gross Domestic Product

The most important measures for the current performance of the economy are gross domestic product (GDP), unemployment rate and inflation rate. GDP is defined as the total dollar value of all the goods and services produced in a year's time, within a country's borders, measured in terms of their market prices. It tells how well the economy is doing. It is measured and reported by the Bureau of Economic Analysis which is an arm of the Department of Commerce. Prior to the year 1991, the measure of the nation's total production as reported by the Department of Commerce was Gross National Product (GNP). The two measures are very similar with minor differences. GDP figures are reported on a quarterly basis and released three times in successive months in advance, preliminary and final forms.

The data is also subject to later revisions. The advance estimate of the GDP is often different from later revisions and this limits the ability of early GDP estimates for prediction of the economic state of the nation. When GDP is accelerating, the economic conditions are improving and when it is decelerating, the economy is deteriorating. When the GDP values for two successive quarters are negative, the country is said to be in recession.

If the GDP adjusted for inflation is reported to grow at an annual rate of 4 percent, it means that the dollar value of all the goods and services produced this year is projected to be 4 percent larger than that of the previous year. If the GDP grows too slowly or actually declines, there would be an increase in unemployment. Similarly, if the GDP grows too rapidly, it would be expected to increase the inflation rate. Note the importance of GDP as a tool for forecasting the future performance of the economy. The economists use this tool to recommend whether the policies for increased growth or slow growth are needed.

14.3 Consumer Spending

It is the amount of money spent by households in an economy. The spending includes both the durable and nondurable items such as food, clothing, transportation, appliances, furniture, entertainment, and medical care, etc. The most important factor affecting consumer spending is the income. If the GDP is rising, more and more unemployed people will be finding jobs. This in turn will lead to increased consumer spending. If the GDP is decreasing, there will be a reduction in consumer spending. The increased consumer spending produces greater demand for the goods and services and leads to economic prosperity.

The consumer spending tends to decline if the consumers' expectations about the future of the economy are not positive and vice versa. If people perceive recession, they cut back on spending. If taxes increase, the amount of spendable income decreases and so does the consumer spending. The decreased consumer spending is negative for investment. With the increase in consumer spending, the demand for goods and services increases. In order to cope with this demand, the companies increase production by hiring more workers and making greater investment in the equipment and technology.

The decrease in corporate taxes and/or the increase in tax incentives for the investment in capital equipment lead to greater investment which is good for the economy.

The total spending in the economy is made up of the consumer spending, investment spending and government spending. The level of the total spending determines the level of total production which determines the GDP. If the total spending increases, the total production and the number of workers employed will increase too. This is good for the economy.

14.4 Unemployment

Each month the Department of Labor releases employment statistics. This includes the number of people employed and unemployed as well as the unemployment rate. This is based on a sample survey of about 60,000 households to determine their employment status in the preceding week. The sample includes households in every part of the country in order to make it representative of the total population. In order to be classified as unemployed, the requirement is that the out-of-work person must be actively seeking work. There are four categories of unemployment:

1. Frictional unemployment which involves people who are temporarily between jobs.
2. Cyclical unemployment which occurs because of the poor economic conditions.
3. Structural unemployment which occurs because of the mismatch between the job openings and the job seekers.
4. Seasonal unemployment which occurs because of the seasonal factors as in farming.

When people are unemployed, they do not have money to buy the discretionary items. This leads to the reduction in demand for such items. This is neither good for the companies producing such items nor for the economy.

14.5 Inflation

When there is a general rise in the prices of goods and services, it is referred to as the inflation. The common measures of the inflation are the producer price index and the consumer price index (which is also sometimes called the cost-of-living index). These indexes are reported by the Department of Labor. The producer price index (PPI) is based on the prices paid by the producers. It is reported as broad and core where the core index excludes the volatile food and energy categories. The consumer price index (CPI) is based on approximately 400 items frequently purchased by the households, known as the typical market basket. Each month the Department of Labor checks the prices of these 400 items in 85 urban areas which include the major parts of the nation. When the aggregate price of the market basket rises, it signals inflation. If some prices rise while others fall, for the inflation the rising prices have to more than offset the falling prices.

The inflation in prices occurs under the following two scenarios:

1. The demand is exceeded by the supply.
2. The price is raised to offset the increased production cost. The latter may be due to the higher prices for labor, raw materials, capital goods, energy, or some other item needed in the production.

The effect of inflation is to decrease the purchasing power of the dollar. When that occurs, it creates a real hardship for the people on fixed income. For example, the inflation more than tripled during the period 1970-1990. That means that a person needed $15,000 in the year 1990 to buy the same amount of goods and services as $5,000 bought in the year 1970. In other words, the money was worth considerably less 20 years later. This shows the need to invest money for growth in order to preserve the same purchasing power.

The inflation is checked by restricting the money supply or increasing the interest rate. Both of these measures have adverse effect on the employment. The reduction in employment curtails consumer spending and so is harmful for the economy.

14.6 Fiscal Policy

It refers to the use of the government's spending and taxing policies so as to influence the economy. The government tinkers with the economy by changing the money supply and/or the tax rates. These measures help to restore the proper level of GDP. If GDP is too high, the economy will experience inflation and if too low, it will suffer from unemployment. Therefore, in order to have a healthy economy, it is necessary to control spending so that the GDP will be neither too high nor too low.

The example of the fiscal policy used to manage the economy is provided by the following succession of events. When President John F. Kennedy took office in 1961, the country was suffering from recession that commenced in the year 1958. His administration adopted the following fiscal policy measures: increased the federal spending on highways and passed the legislation that allowed the businesses to deduct a part of their capital investment on the machinery and the facilities from their taxes. This was followed by a major tax cut in the amount of $11 billion which was signed by President Lyndon Johnson into law in February 1964. In addition to these measures, the economy got boost from the large increases in spending for the Vietnam War. This expansion lasted for a period of more than 8 years (February 1961 – December 1969).

As another example, when President Reagan took office in January 1981, the economy had been suffering from a mild recession. It thus needed a boost which his administration failed to provide for nine months. It was later followed by a meager 5 percent tax cut. At the same time, substantial cuts in federal spending for the domestic programs were made. The lack of federal spending resulted in the severe recession of 1981-1982. When in the year 1982 the tax cuts were substantially increased, the economy started recovering.

14.7 Federal Reserve System

The monetary policy is administered by the Federal Reserve System (often referred to as the Fed). The latter is administered by a Board of Governors and its Chairperson has enormous power in managing the economy. The Federal Reserve System has three levels of organization. The first level consists of the Board of Governors, the Federal Open Market Committee, and the Federal Advisory Council. The second level consists of twelve Federal Reserve Banks scattered around the country, and the third level consists of the thousands of member banks.

The Board of Governors consists of seven members. The members of the Board are appointed by the US President for a 14-year term and the terms of the members are staggered so that a new member is appointed every two years. The President also appoints one of the members as Chairperson of the Board for a term of four years. The Board of Governors is the central policy- making body of the Federal Reserve System. The latter is an independent government agency and the decisions of the Board of Governors do not have to be approved by the President or the Congress. The Board members determine the amount of money made available to the banks for making loans and also the overall interest rate.

The Federal Open Market Committee consists of 12 members: seven members of the Board of Governors and five presidents of the Federal Reserve Banks. The Committee is responsible for directing the buying and selling of government securities in the open market and thereby it influences the interest rates and the availability of credit.

The Federal Advisory Council consists of 12 commercial bankers with one member selected by each of the 12 Federal Reserve Banks. The Council provides a link between the bankers and the Board and has strictly an advisory function.

The Federal Reserve Banks are located in twelve regions of the country. Their activities are coordinated by the Board of Governors. They deal only with banks and other financial institutions but not directly with the public.

The Federal Reserve System serves the following functions:

1. To act as the clearing house for the checks issued and facilitating thereby the credit and debit to accounts.
2. To serve as a fiscal agent for the federal government because the money collected by the treasury from taxes is deposited in the

Federal Reserve Banks and is then disbursed for tax refunds, social security payments, government purchases, etc.

3. To meet the requirements of the paper money in circulation.
4. To hold the required reserves of the banks and other financial institutions.
5. To ensure that the member banks are in compliance with the banking laws and meet the reserve requirements and the loan limits as in effect at any time.
6. To regulate the amount of money in circulation by increasing or decreasing the reserve requirements for banks and/or changing the discount rate. The latter is the rate of interest that the Federal Reserve Banks charge the banks and the financial institutions for loans. An increase in the discount rate is usually followed by a similar increase in the prime rate which is the rate that banks charge their best customers.

14.8 Monetary Policy

Of all the functions stated above, the most important function of the Federal Reserve System is to control the nation's money supply and interest rates in order to achieve the desirable economic conditions. The actions taken by the Fed with regard to this objective are called the monetary policy. The objectives that the Fed attempts to achieve through monetary policy are economic growth, low unemployment and stable prices. The way it works is as follows. When the unemployment is low and the money supply is abundant, the economy heats up resulting in higher inflation. The corrective action by the Fed is to reduce the supply of money by increasing the reserve requirement for banks and/or increasing the discount rate. Since the banks can loan only the money received as deposits less the reserves needed, the money to loan will be less with increased reserve requirement. Because of the increase in discount rate, money will be available at a higher interest rate. These changes in the monetary policy would lead to reduced consumer and business spending and so there will be less inflationary pressure on the economy. This is the example of tight-money policy.

In contrast to the above, if the economy is in recession and unemployment is rising, the Fed will increase the money supply by reducing the reserve requirement and/or reducing the discount rate. These Fed actions in the monetary policy will lead to the money being available more abundantly and cheaply. As a result of these, the consumer and business spending will increase leading to higher employment. This is called the easy-money policy.

In addition to the reserve requirement, the Fed can also pump or squeeze money in the economy through open market operations. This involves buying and selling the US Government Securities by the Fed in the open market (the market open to citizens and businesses). When the Fed buys securities in the open market, the payment that Fed makes ends up in the banks thereby increasing the bank reserves. This means that there is more money available to the banks to loan to their customers. Conversely, when the Fed sells securities in the open market, the buyers pay for these securities from the funds withdrawn from their accounts in banks and so the reserve money in the bank decreases. With the decrease in reserves, the lending capacity of the banks is also decreased. This causes a decrease in the money supply.

The monetary policy affects the people in significant ways. When the money supply is tight, it is difficult to get the loans for appliances, cars and houses, etc. and if the loan is available it will be at higher interest rates. The longer the period of the loan, the more it hurts financially. Conversely, if the money supply is easy, the loans will be easily available and at cheaper interest rates. The change in money supply and/or discount rate affects the interest rate. When the interest rates are low, the returns on bank accounts are also low and vice versa. Thus the Fed monetary policy has a direct effect on us both as the consumers and the investors.

14.9 Economic Downturns and Corrective Measures

The economy is changing all the time and sometimes goes through the extremes. Noteworthy among them is the Great Depression of the 1930s when unemployment rate was 25 percent and the masses were homeless and hungry. The factories were idle because there was no market for the products since people were unemployed and had no money to buy those products. Since there was no demand, the market prices of the goods went down so much that it was not even profitable to produce the goods and sell in the market.

This downturn occurred because the government failed to institute policies to revive the economy. Then there was a severe recession in 1981- 1982. In this economic downturn, the unemployment rate reached 10.7 percent and nearly one-third of the industrial capacity was idle. It was again a failure on the part of our politicians to implement the sound economic policies. In both of these examples, the dangers from high unemployment rate are obvious because if people do not have jobs, they don't have the money to spend. If people can't buy, there is no market for the goods produced by our companies. If the companies become idle, there are no jobs. So there are adverse factors which feed into themselves.

There have been many housing-related downturns. The downturn of 1978 to 1982 was triggered by an abnormally high 30-year fixed mortgage rate of 13.5 percent. The downturn of 2007–2009 was also related to the mortgage but the average mortgage rate of about 6 percent was not the problem. This problem was instead created by the housing boom that resulted from an abnormal demand due to easy money supply. People with bad credits and in no position to make payments on their mortgage were able to borrow the money for homes with prices that their earnings did not justify. Many people signed up for mortgages with low interest rates for the first few years which were to be bumped to higher rates later. The higher rate put the payment beyond the means of these people. Some people bought the homes for speculative purposes because the homes were appreciating fast and so they envisioned cashing on the appreciated values without having to pay at higher mortgage rates. As the defaults increased, the market was stuck with foreclosures that produced a glut of such homes along with the homes newly completed or under completion. Since the builders were stuck with these homes on their books, they dumped them in the market at much cheaper prices thereby producing further glut. This action led to the overall drop in the home values. As a result of this, the people got stuck with homes with the mortgage balances greater than the loan values. This situation prompted these homeowners to walk away and so the lending institutions got stuck with these foreclosed homes on their books. This led to even more glut of the homes in the market. The banks bundled the mortgage securities and sold them as the collateral securities which went in default because the homeowners defaulted.

The general downfall in home values produced a climate in which other homeowners felt insecure because their homes had gone down in value too. All of these factors together with the increased energy and food prices because of high inflation contributed to high consumer debt and considerably reduced consumer spending. With the collapse of Lehman Brothers in September 2008, the banks and the investors reversed their course so that the liquidity dried up. This brought the global financial system to its knees accompanied with massive unemployment. In order to this avert this crisis, the Government reacted aggressively by injecting massive amounts into the financial markets while slashing the interest rates and injecting discretionary spending. The Congress enacted an economic stimulus package of $150 billion dollars which provided cash payments of $600 per adult and $300 per child to most people except those in very high tax brackets. Another legislation to provide government guarantee to the strapped homeowners to refinance their home loans at cheaper rates was also enacted. As a result of these actions, the job market and the economy recovered.

14.10 Economy and the Stock Market

Since businesses are affected by the economy, it obvious that the stock market will be affected by the economy as well. The economy cycles between the periods of economic growth and recession. If growth becomes overheated it results in inflation. This is followed by the tightening of money supply by the Fed which in the extreme results in recession. Thus the economy cycles between inflation and recession. The actions of the Fed and the Government can minimize the impact of inflation and recession but nothing can be done to erase these economic cycles. The National Bureau of Economic Research (NBER) declares officially the peaks and troughs of the business cycle but the information lags badly. This is so because the process of collecting economic data and the revised preliminary estimates of economic activity take time. The stock market perceives these changes and responds well in advance of the changes being declared officially. From the investor's perspective, the key then is to identify the direction in which the economy is headed and then buy or sell into the trend.

An economic cycle may be divided into four periods: the period of early recovery, the period of full recovery, the period of early recession and the period of full recession. In the first period, the consumer expectations and the industrial production start rising while the interest rates are in the process of bottoming out. In this atmosphere, the basic industry and the energy sectors take lead. In the second period, the economy has fully recovered, and the consumer expectations and the productivity levels are falling. The consumer staples and the service sectors do well in this atmosphere. In the third period, consumer expectations fall and the productivity levels are low. The utility and financial sectors do well in this atmosphere. In the fourth period of full recession, the industrial production stays low. The businesses do not increase production unless they see the signs of consumer spending. The cyclical and technology stocks do well in this atmosphere.

14.11 Summary

1. The measures of the economy are gross domestic product (GDP), unemployment rate and inflation rate.
2. GDP is defined as the total dollar value of all the goods produced and services rendered in the country in a year's time. The advance estimate of GDP as the predictor of economy is limited because of the large differences between the estimated and the revised values.
3. Consumer spending refers to the purchase of consumer goods and services by the consumers for their personal use. It increases if the GDP increases and vice versa.
4. The total spending in the economy is made up of the consumer spending, investment spending and government spending.
5. The employment statistics are reported each month by the Department of Labor. These include the number of people employed and unemployed as well as the unemployment rate.
6. There are four kinds of unemployment: frictional, cyclical, structural, and seasonal.
7. The measures of inflation are the consumer price index and the producer price index. They provide the idea of inflation at the consumer and producer levels. Inflation decreases the purchasing power of the dollar over a period of time.
8. The inflation is controlled by restricting the money supply and/or increasing the interest rate.
9. Fiscal policy refers to the policy implemented by the government to control the money supply so as to affect the economy.
10. The monetary policy is implemented by the Federal Reserve System. It involves setting the discount rate and changing the money supply.
11. The economy cycles between the periods of economic growth and recession. The recognition of the stages in the cycle may be used to advantage by the investor.

Concluding Remarks

On the Road to Wealth

The very fact that you bought the book tells me that you are interested in building wealth. The problem may be that you do not have enough money to start. Remember wealth means different things for different people. For Jeff Bezos a hundred dollars bill is a spare change, but for most people it is real money. If you can manage to spare a few hundred dollar bills, pretty soon you will be building wealth. Some of you may wonder how to have spare hundred dollars. If you want to have a secure future, you will need to figure it out. May be you have to cut down on eating in the restaurant, economizing on groceries, skipping on vacation trips, or get a better job. If the latter needs new skills, you have to work on that. Finally remember where there is a will, there is a way. Chapter 1 showed you that you can start with a certificate of deposit in your bank and capitalize on the magic of compounding to build a

small wealth. That opens the door for you to capitalize on more rewarding investments such as bonds and stocks. From there onwards the road is straightforward as follows:

1. Read Chapter 2 and start with the investment in SPY at a brokerage. SPY is the symbol for SPDR S&P 500 Trust which is an ETF designed to track the S&P 500 stock market index. Since SPY deals with the broad spectrum of economy, you do not have to worry with the fluctuations in the specific segments of the economy. Monitor your investment on a regular basis to get used to the daily fluctuation in stock prices. It will increase your interest in the stock market as well.

2. Read Chapter 3 to develop some familiarity with the stock market terminology and to learn how it is relevant to stock market investing.

3. Read Chapter 4 on Financial Statements. Pay attention to the concepts covered in the context of how the business works and how we come up with revenues, earnings, dividends, assets, liabilities, equity, cash flow etc. You should have at least some general idea.

4. Pay special attention to Chapter 5 dealing with the selection and analysis of stocks. Here you learn what to look for in the selection of a company for investment. With so many companies there it is easy to get lost. A simple approach may be to look at the companies that you know by your exposure to the items of general need. Examples are Facebook, Google, Microsoft, Amazon, Home Depot, Johnson and Johnson, MasterCard, Visa, FedEx, etc. The website will help you in narrowing down the list and then analyze as discussed in Chapter 5. Brokerages show their preference but I recommend that you familiarize and use your analysis so that you become familiar with the financial aspects of the companies in which you finally invest. Look at the chart pattern discussed in Chapter 6 on technical analysis to be sure that your timing for investment in the company is right. Chapter 6 enables you to see how the stock has performed and whether it is the right time to invest in a particular stock.

5. Follow your stocks in a spread sheet. Yahoo Finance provides many formats free of charge.

Further Reading

Appel, Gerald, Technical Analysis, Power Tools for Active Investors, Prentice Hall, 2005.

Bogle, John, The Little Book of Common Sense Investing: The Only Way to Guarantee Your Fair Share of Stock Market Returns, Wiley, 2007.

Bouchentouf, Amine, Brian Dolan, Joe Duarte, Mark Galant, Ann C. Logue, Paul Mladjenovic, Kerry Pechter, Barbara Rockefeller, Peter J. Sander and Russell Wild, High-Powered Investing, All-in-One for Dummies, Wiley, 2008.

Buffett, Warren, Letters to Shareholders, www.BerkshireHathway.com.

Dorsey, Pat, The Five Rules for Successful Stock Investing, Wiley, 2004.

Faerber, Esme, All About Stocks, McGraw Hill, 2008.

Faerber, Esme, All about Bonds and Bond Mutual Funds, 2000.

Fisher, Philip, Common Stocks and Uncommon Profits and Other Writings, Wiley, 2003.

Graham, Benjamin, The Intelligent Investor: The definitive book on value investing, First Collins Business Essentials, 2006.

Griffis, Michael and Epsterin, Lita, Trading for Dummies, Wiley, 2009.

Hagstrom, Robert, The Warren Buffett Way, Wiley, 2013.

Horowitz, Andrew, Winning Investor's Guide to Making Money in Any Market, St. Martin's Griffin, 2010.

Jones, Charles P., Investments: Analysis and Management, Wiley, 2004.

Lynch, Peter with John Rothchild, One Up On Wall Street, Simon & Schuster, 2000.

Thau, Annette, The Bond Book: Everything Investors Need to Know About

Treasuries, Municipals, GNMAs, Corporates, Zeros, Bond Funds, Money Market Funds, and More, McGraw-Hill, 2001.

Thomsell, Michael C., Getting Started in Bonds, Wiley, 1991.

Tyson, Eric, Mutual Funds for Dummies, Wiley, 2010.

Wright, Sharon, Getting Started in Bonds, Wiley, 2003.

INDEX

Floating rate bonds Foreign
stocks

Freddie Mac

Free cash flow , Free
cash flow

Full-service brokerage

Full-Service Brokers Fund of
funds

Fundamental analysis Ginnie
Mae

Ginnie Mae mortgage-backed securities (MBSs) Ginnie
Maes

Global Industry Classification Standard (GICS)

Government Agency Securities

Government-sponsored agencies

Government-sponsored enterprises (GSEs Gross
domestic product

Gross profit

Gross profit margin Growth
stocks

HH savings bonds High
Yield Bond

Nano-cap stocks

NASDAQ

Net asset value (NAV)

Net profit margin No-load

fund

NYSE

Open-end funds

Operating margin

Portfolio Aggressive

Portfolio Capital Preservation

PowerShares FTSE RAFI US 1000 ETF

Preferred stock

Producer price index Profit

margin

Putable bond Putable

bonds

R-squared

Redemption fees

Redemption Value

Relative Strength Indicator (RSI)

Resistance level for stock

Return on shareholder equity

Standard and Poor's (S&P) Report Standard
deviation

Statement of Cash Flows

Stochastic Oscillator　,

Stochastic Oscillator Stock
exchange

, Stock exchange , Stock

exchange , Stock exchange,

Stock exchange , Stock

exchange , Stock exchange,

Stock exchange , Stock

exchange , Stock exchange

Stock funds

Stock market indexes Stop
Order

Strategic Asset Allocation

Stripped Bond STRIPS

Student Loan Marketing Corporation (Sallie Mae)

Yield to Maturity (YTM) Zero
Coupon Bond

Zero coupon bonds , Zero
coupon bonds

www.ingramcontent.com/pod-product-compliance
Lightning Source LLC
Chambersburg PA
CBHW041208220326
41597CB00030BA/5099